THE NEW
FISH & SEAFOOD
COOKBOOK

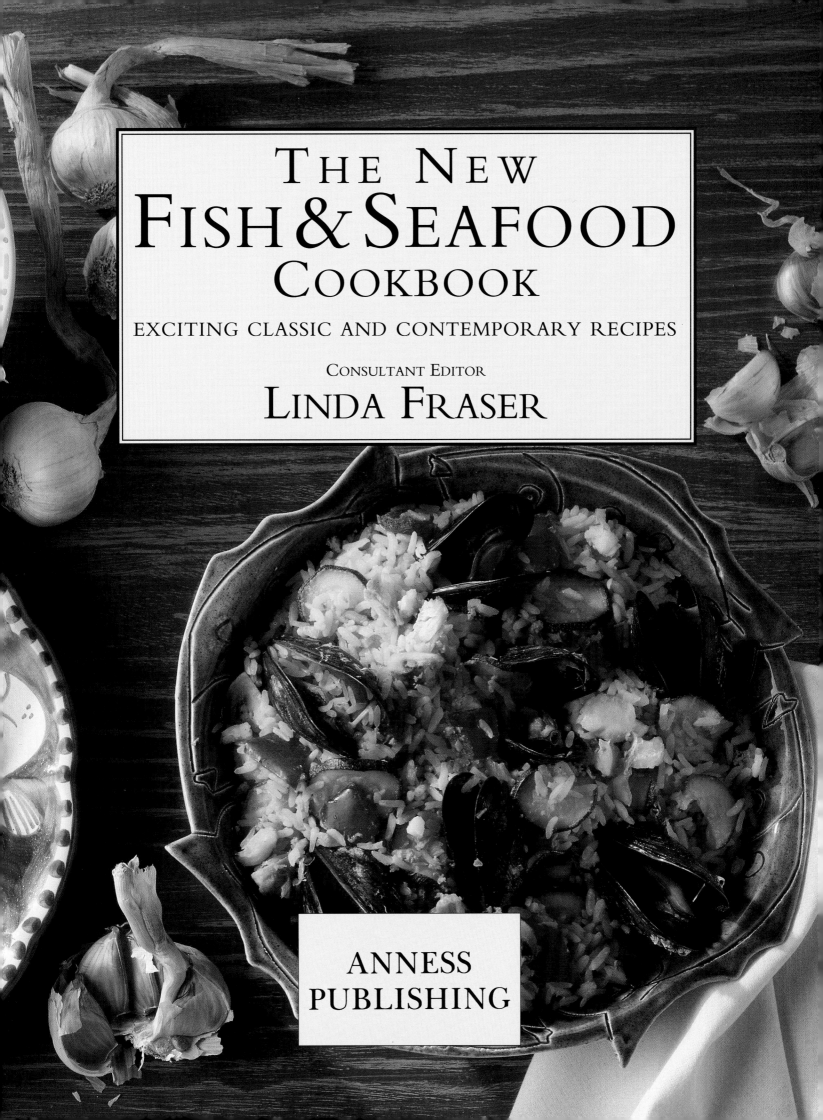

THE NEW
FISH & SEAFOOD
COOKBOOK

EXCITING CLASSIC AND CONTEMPORARY RECIPES

CONSULTANT EDITOR

LINDA FRASER

ANNESS
PUBLISHING

Anness Publishing Limited
Boundary Row Studios
1 Boundary Row
London SE1 8HP

ISBN 0–8317–1144–2

Editorial Director: Joanna Lorenz
Series Editor: Linda Fraser
Designers: Tony Paine and Roy Prescott
Photographers: Steve Baxter, Karl Adamson and Amanda Heywood
Food for Photography: Wendy Lee, Jane Stevenson and Elizabeth Wolf Cohen
Props Stylists: Blake Minton and Kirsty Rawlings

Printed and bound in Singapore

 The apple symbol indicates a low fat, low cholesterol recipe.

CONTENTS

A Look at Fish

In terms of shape and structure, most fish fall into one of two general categories: round fish and flatfish.

Round fish have thicker bodies and many of their bones are attached to their fins. They can be filleted or cut into steaks or cutlets, but all will contain small pin bones.

Flatfish have a flat central bone with a row of bones attached on either side. This simple bone structure makes flatfish easy to fillet. Most are too thin to cut into steaks.

Large fish such as tuna have a thick bone running down the center of their bodies; spiking out from this are four rows of bones that divide the flesh into quarters. These boneless 'loins' are usually sliced into steaks.

The fat content of fish is an important consideration in deciding how to cook it. Lean fish can dry out at high temperatures, so a protective coating is a good idea when frying. When broiling, marinate or baste them. Lean and moderately lean fish are best cooked by moist methods such as steaming, poaching and baking in sauce. Oily fish, however, almost baste themselves during cooking, so they are ideal for baking, broiling and pan-frying.

Texture and flavor are also important in choosing how to prepare fish. If the flavor of the flesh is mild, it is important not to overwhelm it. But fish with rich, distinctively flavored flesh will stand up well to spicy, pungent seasonings.

Fish that are delicate in texture need careful cooking. Pan-frying with a flour coating, steaming and gentle baking are best. However, fish with meaty, dense flesh can be cubed and put on to skewers.

Preparing Whole Fish for Cooking

Most fish have scales and these should be removed before cooking unless the fish is to be filleted or the skin is to be removed before serving. Fish sold by fishmongers will normally be scaled as well as cleaned (eviscerated or drawn), but you can do this yourself, if necessary. Trimming the tail gives a whole fish a neat appearance.

All fish preparation is best done in or near the sink, with cool water running. Salt your hands for a good grip on the fish.

1 **To scale**: grasp the tail firmly and scrap off the scales using a special fish scaler or a knife, working from the tail towards the head. Rinse the fish well. Repeat on the other side.

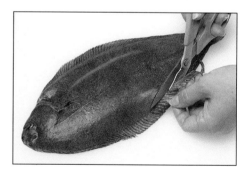

2 **To trim**: for flatfish to be cooked whole, use kitchen scissors to trim off the outer half of the small fin bones all around the fish.

3 For round fish, cut the flesh on both sides of the anal and dorsal (back) fins and pull them out; the small bones attached will come out too. Trim off the other fins.

4 If the fish is to be cooked whole, leave the fins on, or just trim them, because they help keep the shape of the fish.

5 **To trim the tail**: if the tail is to be left on, cut a neat 'V' in the centre with scissors. The fish is now ready for cooking.

BONING FISH

Round fish, such as trout, mackerel and salmon, are normally cleaned by slitting open the belly. It is a simple step on from here to removing the backbone. This leave a bone-free fish and a neat shape for stuffing.

When the boned fish is opened out like a book, or 'butterflied', it is approximately the same thickness throughout for even, quick cooking.

BONING THROUGH THE BACK

An alternative boning method to the one shown here is done from the back rather than the belly. Leave the head and tail on the fish. Set the fish belly down on the work surface and use a sharp knife to slit the skin along one side of the backbone, all the way from the head to the tail. Ease the knife through the slit and work it down the side of the rib cage to detach the bones completely from the flesh. Slit the skin on the other side of the backbone and ease the knife down the rib cage to detach the flesh on that side. With scissors, snip the backbone free at head and tail ends, then lift it out along with the gills and the stomach contents.

---

1 If the head has not already been removed, cut it off by slicing just behind the gills. Remove the tail completely, cutting straight across.

3 If it is possible, lift out the backbone and rib cage in one piece after freeing it with the knife. If it is necessary to cut the backbone out, slide the knife under the bones along one side of the rib cage.

2 Enlarge the belly opening. Set the fish on a board, skin side up, with the belly flaps against the board. Press firmly along the backbone to loosen it. Turn the fish over.

4 Gently ease the knife outward under the rib bones, away from the backbone. Repeat on the other side.

---

5 Lift up the rib cage in one piece and slide the knife under the backbone, to free it from the skin.

6 Run your fingers over the flesh to locate any other bones and pull them out with tweezers.

7 After boning, rinse the fish under cool running water and pat dry with paper towels.

CUTTING FISH FILLETS

Fillets are boneless pieces of fish, and for this reason are very popular. A sharp filleting knife, with its thin, flexible blade, is the tool to use for removing the fillets. Be sure to keep all the bones and trimmings for making stocks.

Round fish are easy to fillet and they produce a boneless piece from each side. Large flatfish are also easy to deal with, although they are filleted slightly differently from round fish and they yield four narrow fillets – two from each side.

FILLETING SMALL FLATFISH

You can take two fillets from smaller flatfish (one from each side): cut behind the head and down the sides of the fish as above, but do not make the central cut. Starting from the head end on one side and working down the fish, cut the flesh away from the rib bones until you reach the center (the backbone). Rotate the fish and repeat on the other side to cut away the whole fillet. Turn the fish over and repeat to cut away the second whole fillet.

---

1 **To fillet a round fish**: lay the fish flat, on its side. First cut off the head. With the tip of the knife, cut through the skin all along the length of the backbone.

2 Working from head to tail and holding the knife almost parallel to the fish, use short strokes to cut one fillet off the rib bones in one piece. Follow the slit cut along the backbone.

3 When you reach the tail, cut across to release the fillet. Repeat the procedure on the other side to remove the other fillet.

4 Run your fingers over the flesh side of each fillet to locate any stray bones. Pull them out with tweezers.

5 **To fillet a flatfish**: lay the fish flat and make a curved cut behind the head, cutting down to but not through the backbone. With the tip of the knife, slit the skin down both sides of the fish where the fin bones meet the rib bones, 'outlining' the fillets, and slit across the tail.

6 Slit straight down the centre line of the fish, from head to tail, cutting down to the backbone. Working from the center at the head end, cut one fillet neatly away from the rib bones on one side. Hold the knife blade almost parallel to the fish and use short strokes.

7 Rotate the fish and cut away the second fillet. Turn the fish over and repeat to remove the two fillets on the other side. Pull out any stray bones with tweezers.

SKINNING FISH FILLETS

Before cooking, dark or tough skin is usually removed from fish fillets. However, if they are to be broiled, the skin helps keep the shape and should not be removed.

GETTING A GRIP ON FISH

If you salt your fingers, you will get a better grip on the tail end so you can hold the skin taut as you cut. This is also a good way to hang on to fish while scaling.

---

1 Lay the fillet flat, skin side down, tail end towards you. Make a small crossways cut through the flesh down to the skin at the tail end.

2 Grip the bit of skin firmly and insert the knife blade so it is almost parallel to the skin, then cut the fillet away. Use a gentle sawing motion and make one continuous cut.

CUTTING FISH STEAKS

Round fish, such as cod or salmon, and large flatfish such as halibut are often cut into steaks for cooking. They are usually about 1–1½ in thick. Steaks cut from the tail end of the fish are smaller, but may contain fewer bones.

1 With a large, sharp knife, slice the fish across, at a right angle to the backbone, into thick slices.

2 If necessary, cut through the backbone with kitchen scissors or a knife with a serrated blade.

TESTING TO DETERMINE WHEN FISH IS COOKED

All seafood cooks quickly. If overcooked it becomes dry and loses its succulent quality. In the case of meaty fish such as tuna and swordfish, it can be unpleasantly chewy. It is therefore worth knowing how to judge when fish is perfectly cooked.

The flesh of raw fish and crustaceans is translucent; it becomes opaque when it is cooked. However, as fish will continue cooking from residual heat, it should be removed from the heat source before it is entirely opaque.

1 To determine whether a fish is cooked, make a small slit in the thickest part. Lift with the knife to look into the opening.

2 The fish is ready when still very slightly translucent in the center or near the bone, but the rest of the flesh is opaque throughout.

PREPARING MUSSELS AND CLAMS

Mollusks such as mussels and clams should be eaten very fresh and must be alive when you buy them and cook them (unless they have been shelled and frozen). You can tell that they are alive if their shells are tightly closed; any shells that are open should close promptly when tapped. Any dead mussels or clams, or any with broken shells, should be discarded.

If you have collected clams yourself, let them stand in a bucket of sea water for several hours, changing the water once or twice. (Do not use fresh water because it will kill the clams.) Add a handful or two of cornmeal or flour to the water to help clean the clams' stomachs. Clams bought from the fish market will already have been purged of sand.

SAILOR'S MUSSELS

Prepare 2–3 quarts live mussels. Steam with 1 cup dry white wine or fish or chicken stock, 1 small chopped onion, 1–2 minced garlic cloves and ½ cup chopped fresh parsley. With a slotted spoon, transfer the opened mussels to large bowls. Add 3 tbsp butter to the cooking liquid and stir until melted, then add pepper. Pour over the mussels. *Serves 4.*

1 Scrub the shells of mussels or clams with a stiff brush and rinse well, either in a large bowl, or under cool running water.

3 **To steam**: put a little dry white wine or water in a large pot, with flavorings as the recipe specifies. Add the mussels or clams, cover tightly and bring to the boil. Steam for 5–10 minutes or until the shells open, shaking the pot occasionally.

5 **To open a live clam**: hold it firmly in one hand, with the hinge of your palm. Insert the side of a clam or oyster knife blade between the shell halves and work it round to cut through the hinge muscle.

2 Before cooking mussels, scrape off any barnacles, then pull off their 'beards' with the help of a small knife. Rinse the mussels well.

4 Serve the mussels or clams in their shells, or shell them before using. Strain the cooking liquid (which will include all the delicious liquor from the shells) and spoon it over the mussels or clams, or use it as the basis for a sauce.

6 Open the shell and cut the clam free of the shell. Do this over a bowl in order to catch all the liquid from the shell.

PREPARING AND DEVEINING SHRIMP

Shrimp can be cooked in their shells, but more often they are peeled first (the shells can be used to make an aromatic stock). The intestinal vein that runs down the back is removed from large shrimp mainly because of its appearance, although if the shrimp are large, the vein may contain grit which makes it unpleasant to eat.

Shrimp are occasionally sold with their heads. These are easily pulled off, and will enhance the flavor of stock make with the shells.

1 Holding the shrimp firmly in one hand, pull off the legs with the fingers of the other hand.

2 Peel the shell away from the body. When you reach the tail, hold the body and pull away the tail; the shell will come off with it. Or, you can leave the tail on the shrimp and just remove the body shell.

3 Make a shallow cut down the center of the curved back of the shrimp. Pull out the black vein with a toothpick or your fingers.

4 **To butterfly shrimp**: cut along the deveining slit to split open the shrimp, without cutting all the way through. Open up the shrimp flat.

5 **To devein shrimp in the shell**: insert a toothpick crosswise in several places along the back where the shell overlaps to lift out the vein.

MAKING FISH STOCK

Fish stock is much quicker to make than meat or poultry stock. Ask your fish merchant for heads, bones and trimmings from white flesh.

MAKES ABOUT 1 QUART

1½lb (heads, bones and trimmings from white fish
1 onion, sliced
2 celery stalks with leaves, chopped
1 carrot, sliced
½ lemon, sliced (optional)
1 bay leaf
a few fresh parsley sprigs
6 black peppercorns
5½ cups water
½ cup dry white wine

1 Rinse the fish heads, bones and trimmings well under cold running water. Put in a stockpot with the vegetables, lemon, if using, the herbs, peppercorns, water and wine. Bring to the boil, skimming the surface frequently, then reduce the heat and simmer for 25 minutes.

2 Strain the stock without pressing down on the ingredients in the strainer. If not using immediately, leave to cool and then refrigerate. Fish stock should be used within 2 days, or it can be frozen for up to 3 months.

SOUPS & APPETIZERS

Fish and seafood make delightful first courses, especially if you are serving a meaty or rich main course. For an informal or family supper, opt for a simple uncooked dish such as Smoked Mackerel and Apple Dip, or Smoked Trout with Cucumber Salad. If the weather is chilly, go for a chunky soup such as Haddock and Broccoli Chowder. For a special occasion you might like to choose Gravadlax Trout.

Gravadlax Trout

Although traditionally done with whole salmon, this marinating treatment also does wonders with small trout, but generally the larger the fish the better. If you ever get locally caught, large lake trout, this is the best thing to do with them.

INGREDIENTS

Serves 4
2 large trout, gutted and heads removed
1 bunch of dill

Marinade ingredients for each 1lb of fish
½ tbsp coarse salt
½ tbsp sugar
½ tbsp crushed peppercorns

For the mustard sauce
1 tsp strong mustard
1 tbsp chopped fresh dill
2 tsp sugar
1 tsp cider vinegar
5 tbsp sour cream

1 Slit the trout from the stomach to the tail in a straight line, then lay each fish on its stomach, opened out, and press firmly along the backbone, down to the tail. Turn over and gently, with the point of a knife, ease out the whole of the backbone in one piece, then pick out any other loose bones.

2 Weigh the fish now and calculate the quantities of marinade seasonings. Lay one fish skin side down in a tight-fitting, non-metallic dish. Wash and dry the dill and place on top.

3 Mix the marinade seasonings together and sprinkle evenly over the dill. Top with the other fish, cover with foil or a dish and place weights evenly on top of the fish.

4 Chill the fish for 48 hours. Turn every 6–12 hours, basting with the marinating liquid.

5 Mix all the sauce ingredients together and chill. Scrape away the dill and peppers from the fish and pat dry. Cut into fillets, or thinly slice the fish horizontally. Serve with hot bread and the mustard sauce.

Smoked Trout with Cucumber Salad

Smoked trout provides an easy and delicious first course. Serve it at room temperature for the best flavor.

INGREDIENTS

Serves 4
1 large cucumber
4 tbsp crème fraîche or strained plain
  yogurt
1 tbsp chopped fresh dill
4 smoked trout fillets
salt and black pepper
dill sprigs, to garnish
crusty whole wheat bread, to serve

1 Peel the cucumber, cut in half lengthwise and scoop out the seeds using a teaspoon. Cut into tiny dice.

2 Put the cucumber in a colander set over a plate and sprinkle with salt. Leave to drain for at least 1 hour to draw out the excess moisture.

3 Rinse the cucumber well, then pat dry on paper towels. Transfer the diced cucumber to a bowl and stir in the crème fraîche or yogurt, chopped dill and some freshly ground pepper. Chill the cucumber salad for about 30 minutes.

4 Arrange the trout fillets on individual plates. Spoon the cucumber and dill salad on one side and grind over a little black pepper. Garnish with dill sprigs and serve with crusty bread.

Haddock and Broccoli Chowder

A warming main-meal soup for hearty appetites.

INGREDIENTS

Serves 4
4 scallions, sliced
1lb new potatoes, diced
1¼ cups fish broth or water
1¼ cups skim milk
1 bay leaf
2 cups broccoli florets, sliced
1lb smoked haddock fillets, skinned
7oz can corn kernels, drained
black pepper
chopped scallions, to garnish

1 Place the scallions and potatoes in a large saucepan and add the broth, milk, and bay leaf. Bring the soup to a boil, then cover the pan and simmer for 10 minutes.

2 Add the broccoli to the pan. Cut the fish into bite-sized chunks and add to the pan with the corn kernels.

3 Season the soup well with black pepper, then cover the pan and simmer for 5 minutes more, or until the fish is cooked through. Remove the bay leaf and scatter over the scallions. Serve hot, with crusty bread.

COOK'S TIP

When new potatoes are not available, old ones can be used, but choose a waxy variety that will not disintegrate.

VARIATIONS

Smoked cod fillets would be equally good in this chowder. If you prefer substitute white cod or haddock fillets for half or all of the smoked fish.

Shrimp and Corn Soup

A warming main-meal soup for hearty appetites.

INGREDIENTS

Serves 4

2 tbsp tablespoons olive oil
1 onion, minced
4 tbsp butter or margarine
¼ cup flour
3 cups fish or chicken stock, or clam juice
1 cup milk
1 cup peeled, cooked small shrimp, deveined if necessary
1½ cups corn kernels (fresh, frozen, or canned)
½ tsp minced fresh dill or thyme
salt
hot pepper sauce
½ cup light cream

1 Heat the olive oil in a large heavy saucepan. Add the onion and cook over a low heat for 8–10 minutes, until softened.

2 Meanwhile, melt the butter or margarine in a separate saucepan. Add the flour and stir until thoroughly blended. Cook for 1–2 minutes. Pour in the stock and milk and stir to blend. Bring to a boil over medium heat and cook 5–8 minutes, stirring frequently.

4 Add the sauce to the shrimp and corn mixture and mix well. Remove 2½ cups of the soup and purée in a blender or food processor. Stir into the rest of the soup in the pan. Season with salt and add hot pepper sauce to taste.

5 Add the cream and stir to blend. Heat the soup almost to boiling point, stirring frequently. Serve hot.

3 Chop the shrimp and add to the onion with the corn and chopped fresh dill or thyme. Cook for about 2–3 minutes over a low heat, stirring occasionally, then set aside.

Smoked Mackerel and Apple Dip

Serve this quick fish dip with tasty, curried dippers.

INGREDIENTS

Serves 6–8

12oz smoked mackerel, skinned and boned
1 eating apple, peeled, cored and cut into chunks
⅔ cup ricotta
pinch paprika or curry powder
salt and black pepper
apple slices, to garnish

For the curried dippers

4 slices white bread, crusts removed
2 tbsp butter, softened
1 tsp curry paste

1 Place the smoked mackerel in a food processor with the apple, ricotta and seasonings.

2 Blend for about 2 minutes or until the mixture is really smooth. Check the seasoning, then transfer to a small serving dish and chill.

3 Preheat the oven to 400°F. To make the curried dippers, place the bread on a baking sheet. Blend the butter and curry paste thoroughly, then spread over the bread.

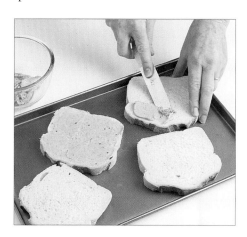

4 Cook the bread in the oven for about 10 minutes, or until crisp and golden. Cut into fingers and serve, while still warm, with the mackerel dip, garnished with the apple slices.

COOK'S TIP

Instead of using plain sliced bread, you could try other breads for the dippers – Italian ciabatta, rye, or pita breads would be excellent.

Salmon Rillettes

INGREDIENTS

Serves 6

12oz salmon fillets
¾ cup butter, softened
1 celery stalk, finely chopped
1 leek, white part only, finely chopped
1 bay leaf
⅔ cup dry white wine
4oz smoked salmon trimmings
generous pinch of ground mace
4 tbsp ricotta
salt and black pepper
salad leaves, to serve

1 Lightly season the salmon. Melt 2 tbsp of the butter in a medium sauté pan. Add the celery and leek and cook for about 5 minutes. Add the salmon and bay leaf and pour over the wine. Cover and cook for about 15 minutes until the fish is tender.

2 Strain the cooking liquid into a pan and boil until reduced to about 2 tbsp. Cool. Meanwhile, melt 4 tbsp of the remaining butter and gently cook the smoked salmon until it turns pale pink. Leave to cool.

3 Remove the skin and any bones from the salmon fillets. Flake the flesh into a bowl and add the reduced, cooled cooking liquid.

4 Beat in the remaining butter, the mace and ricotta. Break up the smoked salmon trimmings and fold into the mixture with the pan juices. Taste and adjust the seasoning.

5 Spoon the salmon mixture into a dish or terrine and smooth the top level. Cover and chill for up to 2 days.

6 To serve the salmon rillettes, shape the mixture into oval quenelles using two dessert spoons and arrange on individual plates with the salad leaves. Accompany with brown bread or wheat crackers, if you like.

Beet and Herring Salad

This colorful salad uses fresh beets – too often underrated.

INGREDIENTS

Serves 4–6

12oz cooked beets, skinned and thickly sliced
2 tbsp vinaigrette dressing
4 pickled herrings, drained
12oz cooked waxy salad potatoes, thickly sliced
½ small red onion, thinly sliced and separated
⅔ cup sour cream
2 tbsp snipped fresh chives
dark rye bread, to serve

1 Mix the sliced beets with the vinaigrette dressing. Arrange the herrings on individual plates with the beets, potatoes and onion rings.

2 Add a generous spoonful of the sour cream to each serving and sprinkle with snipped fresh chives. Serve with dark rye bread.

Garlic Shrimp in Filo Tartlets

Tartlets made with crisp layers of filo pastry and filled with garlic shrimp make a tempting and unusual dinner-party appetizer.

INGREDIENTS

Serves 4

For the tartlets

4 tbsp butter, melted
2–3 large sheets filo pastry

For the filling

½ cup butter
2–3 garlic cloves, crushed
1 red chili, seeded and chopped
12oz cooked, peeled shrimp
2 tbsp chopped fresh parsley or snipped fresh chives
salt and black pepper

1 Preheat the oven to 400°F. Brush four individual 3in pie pans with melted butter.

2 Cut the filo pastry into twelve 4in squares and brush them with the melted butter.

3 Place three squares inside each pan, overlapping them at slight angles and carefully frilling the edges and points while forming a good hollow in each center. Bake for 10–15 minutes, until crisp and golden. Cool slightly and remove from the pans.

4 Meanwhile, make the filling. Melt the butter in a large frying pan, then add the garlic, chili and shrimp and fry quickly for 1–2 minutes to warm through. Stir in the parsley or chives and season with salt and pepper.

5 Spoon the shrimp filling into the tartlets and serve at once.

COOK'S TIP

Use fresh filo pastry, rather than frozen, then wrap and freeze any leftover sheets.

Italian Fish Soup

INGREDIENTS

Serves 4

2 tbsp olive oil
1 onion, thinly sliced
a few saffron threads
1 tsp dried thyme
large pinch of cayenne pepper
2 garlic cloves, finely chopped
2 x 14oz cans peeled tomatoes, drained and chopped
¾ cup dry white wine
8 cups fish stock
12oz white, skinless fish fillets, cut into pieces
1lb monkfish, membrane removed, cut into pieces
1lb mussels in shell, thoroughly scrubbed
8oz small squid, cleaned and cut in rings
2 tbsp chopped fresh parsley
salt and black pepper
thickly sliced bread, to serve

1 Heat the oil in a large, heavy-based saucepan. Add the onion, saffron, thyme, cayenne pepper and salt. Stir well and cook over a low heat for 8–10 minutes, until soft. Add the garlic and cook for a further 1 minute.

2 Stir in the tomatoes, wine and fish stock. Bring to a boil and boil for 1 minute, then reduce the heat and simmer for 15 minutes.

3 Add the fish fillet and monkfish pieces to the pan and simmer gently for a further 3 minutes.

4 Add the mussels and squid and simmer for about 2 minutes, until the mussels open. Stir in the parsley. Season with salt and pepper.

5 Ladle into warmed soup bowls and serve immediately, with bread.

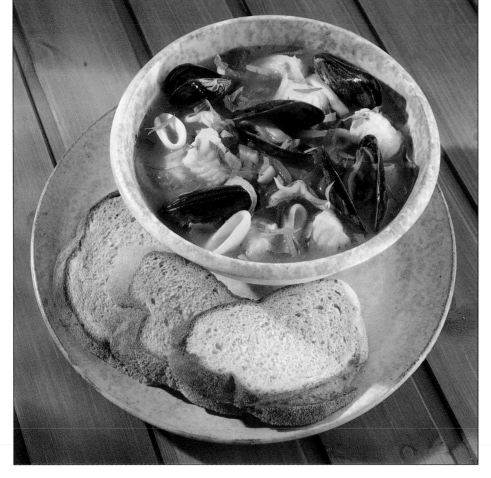

Whitebait with Herb Sandwiches

Whitebait are the tiny fry of sprats or herring. Add enough cayenne pepper to make them spicy hot.

INGREDIENTS

Serves 4
unsalted butter, for spreading
6 slices whole grain bread
6 tbsp chopped fresh mixed herbs, such as parsley, chervil and chives
1lb whitebait, defrosted if frozen
5 tbsp flour
1 tbsp chopped fresh parsley
salt and cayenne pepper
groundnut oil, for deep-frying
parsley sprigs and lemon slices, to garnish

1 Butter the bread slices. Sprinkle the herbs over three of the slices, then top with the remaining slices of bread. Remove the crusts and cut each sandwich into eight triangles. Cover with plastic wrap and set aside.

2 Rinse the whitebait thoroughly. Drain and pat dry on paper towels.

3 Put the flour, chopped parsley, salt and cayenne pepper into a large plastic bag and shake to mix. Add the whitebait and toss gently in the seasoned flour until lightly coated. Heat the oil in a deep-fat fryer to 350°F.

4 Fry the fish in batches for 2–3 minutes, until golden and crisp. Lift out of the oil and drain on paper towels. Keep warm in the oven until all the fish are cooked.

5 Sprinkle the whitebait with salt and more cayenne pepper and garnish with the parsley and lemon slices. Serve at once with the herb sandwiches.

Pasta with Scallops in Tomato Sauce

INGREDIENTS

Serves 4

1lb pasta, such as fettucine
   or linguine
2 tbsp olive oil
2 garlic cloves, finely chopped
1lb scallops, sliced in half
   horizontally
2 tbsp chopped basil
salt and black pepper
fresh basil sprigs, to garnish

For the sauce

2 tbsp olive oil
½ onion, finely chopped
1 garlic clove, finely chopped
salt, to taste
2 x 14oz cans peeled tomatoes

1 To make the sauce, heat the oil in a non-stick frying pan. Add the onion, garlic and a little salt, and cook over a medium heat for about 5 minutes, until just softened, stirring occasionally.

2 Add the tomatoes, with their juice, and crush with a fork. Bring to the boil, then reduce the heat and simmer gently for 15 minutes. Remove the pan from the heat and set aside.

3 Bring a large pan of salted water to a boil. Add the pasta and cook until just tender to the bite, according to instructions on the package.

4 Meanwhile, combine the oil and garlic in another non-stick frying pan and cook for about 30 seconds, until just sizzling. Add the scallops and ½ tsp salt and cook over a hgh heat for about 3 minutes, tossing, until the scallops are cooked through.

5 Add the scallops to the tomato sauce. Season with salt and pepper, then stir gently and keep warm.

6 Drain the pasta, rinse under hot water, and drain again. Add the scallop sauce and the basil and toss thoroughly. Serve immediately, garnished with fresh basil sprigs.

Broiled Garlic Mussels

INGREDIENTS

Serves 4

3–3½lb live mussels
½ cup dry white wine
4 tbsp butter
2 shallots, finely chopped
2 garlic cloves, crushed
6 tbsp dried white
  bread crumbs
4 tbsp chopped fresh mixed herbs,
  such as flat leaf parsley, basil and
  oregano
2 tbsp freshly grated Parmesan
  cheese
salt and black pepper
fresh basil leaves, to garnish

1 Scrub the mussels well under cold running water. Remove the beards and discard any mussels that are open.

2 Place the mussels in a large pan with the wine. Cover the pan and cook over a high heat, shaking the pan occasionally for 5–8 minutes, until the mussels have opened.

3 Strain the mussels and reserve the cooking liquid. Discard any mussels that still remain closed.

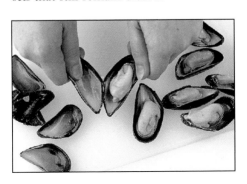

4 Allow the mussels to cool slightly, then remove and discard the top half of each shell, leaving the mussels on the remaining halves.

5 Melt the butter in a pan and fry the shallots until softened. Add the garlic and cook for 1–2 minutes.

6 Stir in the bread crumbs and cook, stirring until lightly browned. Remove the pan from the heat and stir in the herbs. Moisten with a little of the reserved mussel liquid, then season to taste with salt and pepper.

7 Spoon the bread crumb mixture over the mussels in their shells and arrange on baking sheets. Sprinkle with the grated Parmesan.

8 Cook the mussels under a hot broiler in batches for about 2 minutes, until the topping is nicely crisp and golden. Keep the cooked mussels warm in a low oven while broiling the remainder. Garnish with fresh basil leaves and serve hot.

Sole Goujons with Lime Mayonnaise

This simple dish can be rustled up very quickly. It makes an excellent light lunch or supper.

INGREDIENTS

Serves 4
scant 1 cup good-quality
　mayonnaise
1 small garlic clove, crushed
2 tsp capers, rinsed and chopped
2 tsp chopped gherkins
finely grated rind of ½ lime
2 tsp lime juice
1 tbsp chopped fresh coriander
1½lb sole fillets, skinned
2 eggs, beaten
2 cups fresh white bread
　crumbs
oil, for deep-frying
salt and black pepper
lime wedges, to serve

1 To make the lime mayonnaise, mix together the mayonnaise, garlic, capers, gherkins, lime rind and juice and chopped coriander. Season with salt and pepper. Transfer to a serving bowl and chill until required.

2 Cut the sole fillets into finger-length strips. Dip into the beaten egg, then into the bread crumbs.

3 Heat the oil in a deep-fat fryer to 350°F. Add the fish in batches and fry until golden brown and crisp. Drain on paper towels.

4 Pile the goujons on to warmed serving plates and serve with the lime wedges for squeezing over. Pass the sauce round separately.

Spicy Fish Rösti

Serve these fish cakes crisp and hot for lunch with a mixed salad.

INGREDIENTS

Serves 4
12oz large, firm waxy
　potatoes
12oz salmon or cod fillet, skinned
　and boned
3–4 scallions, finely chopped
1 tsp grated fresh ginger root
2 tbsp chopped fresh
　coriander
2 tsp lemon juice
2–3 tbsp sunflower oil
salt and cayenne pepper
lemon wedges, to serve
coriander sprigs, to garnish

1 Cook the potatoes with their skins on in a pan of boiling salted water for 10 minutes. Drain and leave to cool for a few minutes.

2 Meanwhile, finely chop the salmon or cod fillet and put into a bowl. Stir in the chopped scallions, grated ginger root, chopped coriander and lemon juice. Season to taste with salt and cayenne pepper.

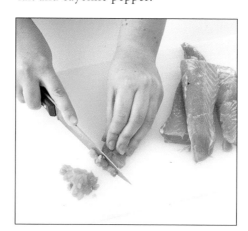

3 When the potatoes are cool enough to handle, peel off the skins and grate the potatoes coarsely. Gently stir the grated potato into the fish mixture.

4 Form the fish mixture into 12 cakes, pressing the mixture together and leaving the edges slightly rough.

5 Heat the oil in a large frying pan, and, when hot, fry the fish cakes a few at a time for 3 minutes on each side, until golden brown and crisp. Drain on paper towels. Serve hot with lemon wedges for squeezing over. Garnish with sprigs of coriander.

Chili Shrimp

This delightful, spicy combination makes a lovely light first course for a casual supper. Serve with rice, noodles or freshly cooked pasta and a leafy salad.

INGREDIENTS

Serves 3–4
3 tbsp olive oil
2 shallots, chopped
2 garlic cloves, chopped
1 fresh red chili, chopped
1lb ripe tomatoes, peeled, seeded and
    chopped
1 tbsp tomato paste
1 bay leaf
1 thyme sprig
6 tbsp dry white wine
1lb cooked, peeled large shrimp
salt and black pepper
coarsely torn basil leaves, to garnish

1 Heat the oil in a pan, then add the shallots, garlic and chili and fry until the garlic starts to brown.

2 Add the tomatoes, tomato paste, bay leaf, thyme, wine and seasoning. Bring to a boil, then reduce the heat and cook gently for about 10 minutes, stirring occasionally, until the sauce has thickened. Discard the herbs.

3 Stir the shrimp into the sauce and heat through for a few minutes. Taste and adjust the seasoning. Scatter over the basil leaves and serve at once.

COOK'S TIP

For a milder flavor, remove all the seeds from the chili.

Scallops with Ginger

Scallops are at their best at this time of year. Try to find ones with the coral attached, as it is colorful and delicious.

INGREDIENTS

Serves 4
8–12 shelled scallops
3 tbsp butter
1in piece fresh ginger root,
    finely chopped
1 bunch scallions, diagonally
    sliced
4 tbsp white vermouth
1 cup crème fraîche or heavy cream
salt and black pepper
chopped fresh parsley, to garnish

1 Remove the tough muscle opposite the coral on each scallop. Separate the coral and cut the white part of the scallop in half horizontally.

2 Melt the butter in a frying pan. Add the scallops, including the corals, and sauté for about 2 minutes until lightly browned. Take care not to overcook the scallops as this will toughen them.

3 Lift out the scallops with a slotted spoon and transfer to a warmed serving dish. Keep warm.

4 Add the ginger and scallions to the pan and stir-fry for 2 minutes. Pour in the vermouth and allow to bubble until it has almost evaporated. Stir in the crème fraîche or cream and cook until the sauce has thickened. Taste and adjust the seasoning.

5 Pour the sauce over the scallops, sprinkle with parsley and serve.

LIGHT LUNCHES

When you are looking for simple dishes to cook, fish and seafood make excellent choices. For family meals, Parsley Fish Cakes or Hoki Balls in Tomato Sauce are easy no-nonsense fare, and in the summer kabobs made with mackerel or monkfish are an appealing way to serve fish to children. If you have friends round, treat them to spicy hot Cajun fish, or a quick and easy pasta dish such as Tagliatelle with Saffron Mussels or Spaghetti with Seafood Sauce.

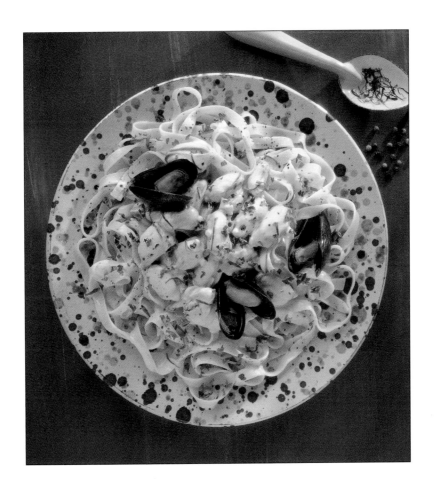

Kashmir Coconut Fish Curry

INGREDIENTS

Serves 4

2 tbsp vegetable oil
2 onions, sliced
1 green bell pepper, seeded and sliced
1 garlic clove, crushed
1 dried chili, seeded and chopped
1 tsp ground coriander
1 tsp ground cumin
½ tsp ground turmeric
½ tsp hot chili powder
½ tsp garam masala
1 tbsp flour
4oz creamed coconut, chopped
1½lb haddock fillets, skinned
  and chopped
4 tomatoes, skinned, seeded
  and chopped
1 tbsp lemon juice
2 tbsp ground almonds
2 tbsp heavy cream
fresh coriander sprigs, to garnish
naan bread and boiled rice, to serve

1 Heat the oil in a large saucepan and add the onions, pepper and garlic. Cook for 6–7 minutes, until the onions and pepper have softened. Stir in the chopped dried chili, all the ground spices, the chili powder, garam masala and flour, and cook for 1 minute.

2 Dissolve the coconut in 2½ cups boiling water and stir into the spicy vegetable mixture. Bring to a boil, cover and then simmer gently for about 6 minutes.

3 Add the fish and tomatoes and cook for about 5–6 minutes, or until the fish has turned opaque. Uncover and gently stir in the lemon juice, ground almonds and cream. Season well, garnish with coriander and serve with naan bread and rice.

—— COOK'S TIP ——

Replace the haddock with any firm fleshed white fish such as cod or whiting. Stir in a few cooked, peeled shrimp, if you like.

Mussels with Wine and Garlic

This famous French dish is traditionally known as *Moules Marinières*.

INGREDIENTS

Serves 4

4lb (about 4 pints) fresh
  mussels in shells
1 tbsp oil
2 tbsp butter
1 small onion or 2 shallots, finely
  chopped
2 garlic cloves, finely chopped
⅔ cup dry white wine or
  apple cider
fresh parsley sprigs
black pepper
2 tbsp chopped fresh parsley,
  to garnish
French bread, to serve

1 Check that the mussels are closed. (Throw away any that are cracked or won't close when tapped.) Scrape the shells under cold running water and pull off the hairy beards attached to the hinges of the shells. Rinse well in two or three changes of water.

2 Heat the oil and butter in a large pan, add the onion or shallots and garlic and fry for 3–4 minutes.

3 Pour on the wine or cider and add the parsley sprigs. Stir well, bring to the boil, then add the mussels. Cover and cook for about 5–7 minutes, shaking the pan once or twice until the shells open (throw away any that have not).

4 Serve the mussels and their juices sprinkled with the chopped parsley and a few grinds of black pepper. Accompany with hot French bread.

Omelette Arnold Bennett

After creating this dish while staying at London's Savoy Hotel, the author, Arnold Bennett, insisted that chefs around the world, wherever he stayed, cooked it for him.

INGREDIENTS

Serves 2

6oz smoked haddock fillet, poached
   and drained
4 tbsp butter, diced
¾ cup whipping or heavy cream
4 eggs, separated
generous ½ cup grated sharp Cheddar
   cheese
salt and black pepper

1 Discard the haddock skin and any bones and flake the flesh.

2 Melt half the butter in 4 tbsp of the cream in a fairly small non-stick saucepan, then lightly stir in the fish. Cover, remove from the heat and leave the mixture to cool.

3 Stir together the egg yolks, 1 tbsp of the cream and pepper, to taste, then lightly stir in the fish mixture. In a separate bowl, mix together the cheese and the remaining cream.

4 Whisk the egg whites until stiff, then fold into the fish mixture.

5 Heat the remaining butter in an omelette pan, add the fish mixture and cook until browned underneath. Pour over the cheese mixture, then broil until golden and bubbling.

Parsley Fish Cakes

For extra-special fish cakes, you could use cooked fresh – or drained, canned – salmon.

INGREDIENTS

Serves 4

1lb cooked mashed potatoes
1lb cooked mixed white and smoked
   fish such as haddock
   or cod, flaked
2 tbsp butter, diced
3 tbsp chopped fresh parsley
1 egg, separated
1 egg, beaten
about 1 cup fine bread crumbs made
   with one day old bread
black pepper
vegetable oil, for frying

1 Place the potatoes in a bowl and beat in the fish, butter, parsley and egg yolk. Season with pepper.

2 Divide the fish mixture into eight equal portions, then, with floured hands, form each into a flat cake.

3 Beat the remaining egg white with the whole egg. Dip each fish cake in the beaten egg, then in bread crumbs.

4 Heat the oil in a frying pan, then fry the fish cakes for about 3–5 minutes on each side, until crisp and golden. Drain on paper towels and serve hot with a crisp salad.

Warm Salmon Salad

Light and fresh, this salad is perfect at this time of year. Serve it immediately, or you'll find the salad leaves will lose their bright color and texture.

INGREDIENTS

Serves 4
1lb salmon fillet, skinned
2 tbsp sesame oil
grated rind of ½ orange
juice of 1 orange
1 tsp Dijon mustard
1 tbsp chopped fresh tarragon
3 tbsp groundnut oil
4oz fine green beans, trimmed
6oz mixed salad leaves, such as young
   spinach leaves, radicchio and frisée
1 tbsp toasted sesame seeds
salt and black pepper

1 Cut the salmon into bite-sized pieces, then make the dressing. Mix together the sesame oil, orange rind and juice, mustard, chopped tarragon and seasoning in a bowl. Set aside.

2 Heat the groundnut oil in a frying pan. Add the salmon pieces and fry for 3–4 minutes, until lightly browned but still tender inside.

3 While the salmon is cooking, blanch the green beans in boiling salted water for about 5–6 minutes, until tender yet crisp.

4 Add the dressing to the salmon, toss together gently and cook for 30 seconds. Remove the pan from the heat.

5 Arrange the salad leaves on serving plates. Drain the beans and toss over the leaves. Spoon over the salmon and cooking juices and serve immediately, sprinkled with the sesame seeds.

Sautéed Salmon with Cucumber

Cucumber is the classic accompaniment to salmon. Here it is served hot – be careful not to overcook the cucumber, or the texture will be lost.

INGREDIENTS

Serves 4
1lb salmon fillet, skinned
3 tbsp butter
2 scallions, chopped
½ cucumber, seeded and cut into strips
4 tbsp dry white wine
½ cup crème fraîche or heavy cream
2 tbsp snipped fresh chives
2 tomatoes, peeled, seeded and diced
salt and black pepper

1 Cut the salmon into about 12 thin slices, then cut across into strips.

2 Melt the butter in a large sauté pan, add the salmon and sauté for 1–2 minutes. Remove the salmon strips using a slotted spoon and set aside.

3 Add the scallions to the pan and cook for 2 minutes. Stir in the cucumber and sauté for 1–2 minutes, until hot. Remove the cucumber and keep warm with the salmon.

4 Add the wine to the pan and let it bubble until well reduced. Stir in the cucumber, crème fraîche or cream, 1 tbsp of the chives and seasoning. Return the salmon to the pan and warm gently. Sprinkle over the tomatoes and remaining chives. Serve at once.

Thai Shrimp Salad

This salad has the distinctive flavor of lemon grass, the bulbous grass used widely in South-east Asian cooking.

INGREDIENTS

Serves 4 as an appetizer
9oz cooked, peeled extra large
  tiger shrimp
1 tbsp oriental fish sauce
2 tbsp lime juice
½ tsp brown sugar
1 small fresh red chili, finely chopped
1 scallion, finely chopped
1 small garlic clove, crushed
1in piece fresh lemon grass,
  finely chopped
2 tbsp chopped fresh coriander
3 tbsp dry white wine
8–12 Boston lettuce leaves, to serve
fresh coriander sprigs, to garnish

1 Place the tiger shrimp in a bowl and add all the remaining ingredients. Stir well, cover and leave to marinate in the fridge for 2–3 hours, mixing and turning the shrimp occasionally.

2 Arrange two or three of the lettuce leaves on each of four individual serving plates.

3 Spoon the shrimp salad into the lettuce leaves. Garnish with fresh coriander and serve at once.

COOK'S TIP

If you find raw shrimp, cook them in boiling water until pink and use instead of the cooked shrimp.

Cajun Spiced Fish

Cajun blackened fish is a speciality of Paul Prudhomme, a chef from New Orleans. Fillets of fish are coated with an aromatic blend of herbs and spices and pan-fried in butter.

INGREDIENTS

Serves 4
1 tsp dried thyme
1 tsp dried oregano
1 tsp ground black pepper
¼ tsp cayenne pepper
2 tsp paprika
½ tsp garlic salt
4 tail end pieces of cod fillet
  (about 6oz each)
6 tbsp butter
½ red bell pepper, sliced
½ green bell pepper, sliced
fresh thyme, to garnish
broiled tomatoes and sweet potato
  purée, to serve

1 Place all the herbs and spices in a bowl and mix well. Dip the fish fillets in the spice mixture until lightly coated.

2 Heat 2 tbsp of the butter in a large frying pan, add the peppers and fry for 4–5 minutes, until softened. Remove the peppers and keep warm.

3 Add the remaining butter to the pan and heat until sizzling. Add the cod fillets and fry on a moderate heat for 3–4 minutes on each side, until they are browned and cooked.

4 Transfer the fish to a warmed serving dish, surround with the peppers and garnish with thyme. Serve the spiced fish with some broiled tomatoes and sweet potato purée.

COOK'S TIP

This blend of herbs and spices can be used to flavor any fish steaks or fillets and could also be used to jazz up pan-fried shrimp.

Tagliatelle with Saffron Mussels

Mussels in a saffron sauce are served with tagliatelle in this recipe, but you can use any other pasta.

INGREDIENTS

Serves 4

4–4½lb live mussels
⅔ cup dry white wine
2 shallots, chopped
12oz dried tagliatelle
2 tbsp butter
2 garlic cloves, crushed
1 cup heavy cream
generous pinch of saffron strands
1 egg yolk
salt and black pepper
2 tbsp chopped fresh parsley,
  to garnish

1 Scrub the mussels well under cold running water. Remove the beards and discard any mussels that are open.

2 Place the mussels in a large pan with the wine and shallots. Cover and cook over a high heat, shaking the pan occasionally, for 5–8 minutes until the mussels have opened. Drain the mussels, reserving the liquid. Discard any that remain closed. Shell all but a few of the mussels and keep warm.

3 Bring the reserved cooking liquid to a boil, then reduce by half. Strain into a cup to remove any grit.

4 Cook the tagliatelle in a large pan of boiling salted water for about 10 minutes, until *al dente*.

5 Meanwhile, melt the butter in a pan and fry the garlic for 1 minute. Pour in the mussel liquid, cream and saffron strands. Heat gently until the sauce thickens slightly. Remove the pan from the heat and stir in the egg yolk, shelled mussels and seasoning to taste.

6 Drain the tagliatelle and transfer to warmed serving bowls. Spoon the sauce over and sprinkle with chopped parsley. Garnish with the mussels in shells and serve at once.

Spaghetti with Seafood Sauce

The Italian name for this tomato-based sauce is *marinara*.

INGREDIENTS

Serves 4

3 tbsp olive oil
1 medium onion, chopped
1 garlic clove, finely chopped
8oz spaghetti
2½ cups crushed tomatoes
1 tbsp tomato paste
1 tsp dried oregano
1 bay leaf
1 tsp sugar
1 cup cooked, peeled baby shrimp
   (rinsed well if canned)
1 cup cooked, peeled large shrimp
1½ cups cooked clams or mussels
   (rinsed well if canned or bottled)
1 tbsp lemon juice
3 tbsp chopped fresh parsley
2 tbsp butter
salt and black pepper
4 whole cooked large shrimp,
   to garnish

1 Heat the oil in a pan and add the onion and garlic. Fry over a moderate heat for 6–7 minutes, until the onion has softened.

2 Meanwhile, cook the spaghetti in a large pan of boiling salted water for 10–12 minutes until *al dente*.

3 Stir the crushed tomatoes, paste, oregano, bay leaf and sugar into the onions and season well. Bring to a boil, then simmer for 2–3 minutes.

4 Add the shellfish, lemon juice and 2 tbsp of the parsley. Stir well, then cover and cook for 3–5 minutes.

5 Meanwhile, drain the spaghetti when it is ready and add the butter to the pan. Return the drained spaghetti to the pan and toss in the butter. Season well.

6 Divide the spaghetti among four warmed plates and top with the seafood sauce. Sprinkle with the remaining 1 tbsp chopped parsley, garnish with whole shrimp and then serve immediately.

Herrings with Walnut Stuffing

Ask the fishmonger to prepare the fish – mackerel can be used if herrings are not available.

INGREDIENTS

Serves 4
2 tbsp butter
1 onion, finely chopped
6 tbsp fresh white bread crumbs
½ cup shelled walnuts, toasted and chopped
finely grated rind of ½ lemon
1 tbsp lemon juice
2 tsp whole grain mustard
3 tbsp mixed chopped fresh herbs, such as sage, thyme and parsley
4 herrings, about 10oz each, without heads and tails, boned
salt and black pepper
lemon wedges and flat leaf parsley sprigs, to garnish

1 Preheat the oven to 375°F. Melt the butter in a frying pan and gently fry the onion for about 10 minutes until golden.

2 Stir in the bread crumbs, chopped walnuts, lemon rind and juice, mustard and herbs. Mix together, then season with salt and pepper to taste.

3 Open out the herring fillets and divide the stuffing among them. Fold the herrings back in half and slash the skin several times on each side.

4 Arrange the herrings in a lightly greased shallow baking pan and bake for 20–25 minutes. Serve hot, garnished with lemon wedges and parsley sprigs.

Trout with Mushroom Sauce

INGREDIENTS

Serves 4
8 trout fillets
seasoned flour
6 tbsp butter
1 garlic clove, chopped
2 tsp chopped fresh sage
12oz mixed wild or cultivated mushrooms
6 tbsp dry white wine
1 cup heavy cream
salt and black pepper
fresh sage sprigs, to garnish

COOK'S TIP

Use a large sharp knife to ease the skin from the trout fillets, then pull out any bones from the flesh – a pair of tweezers makes easy work of this fiddly task!

---

1 Remove the skin from the trout fillets, then carefully remove any bones.

2 Lightly dust the trout fillets on both sides in the seasoned flour, shaking off any excess.

3 Melt the butter in a large frying pan, add the trout fillets and fry gently over a moderate heat for 4–5 minutes, turning once. Remove from the pan and keep warm.

4 Add the garlic, sage and mushrooms to the pan and fry until softened.

5 Pour in the wine and boil briskly to allow the alcohol to evaporate. Stir in the cream and seasoning.

6 Serve the trout fillets on warmed plates with the sauce spooned over. Garnish with a few fresh sage sprigs, if you like.

Fish Balls in Tomato Sauce

This quick meal is a good choice for young children, as you can guarantee no bones. If you like, add a dash of chili sauce.

INGREDIENTS 🍎

Serves 4

1lb white fish fillets such as cod or
    flounder, skinned
4 tbsp fresh whole wheat bread crumbs
2 tbsp snipped fresh chives or scallions
14oz can chopped tomatoes
¾ cup button mushrooms, sliced
salt and black pepper

1 Cut the fish fillets into large chunks and place in a food processor. Add the whole-wheat bread crumbs and chives or scallions. Season to taste with salt and pepper, and process until the fish is finely chopped but still has some texture left.

2 Divide the fish mixture into about 16 even-sized pieces, then shape them into balls with your hands.

3 Place the tomatoes and mushrooms in a wide saucepan and cook over medium heat until boiling. Add the fish balls, cover and simmer for about 10 minutes, until cooked. Serve hot.

— VARIATION —

The fish balls can be prepared several hours in advance if covered and kept in the refrigerator.

— COOK'S TIP —

Instead of using a can of chopped tomatoes and fresh mushrooms, you could substitute a jar of ready-made tomato and mushroom sauce. Just add the fish balls and simmer for 10 minutes.

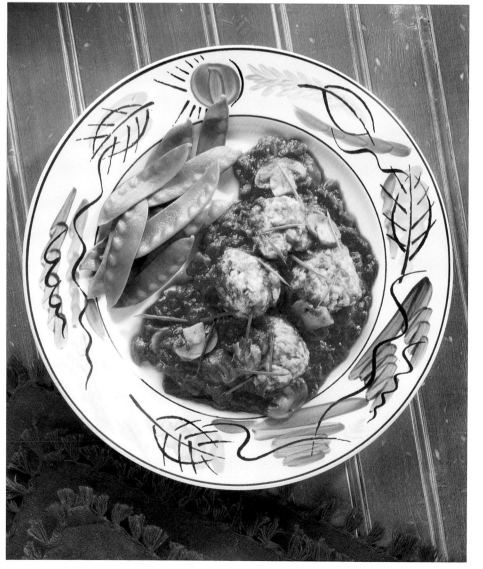

Tuna and Corn Fish Cakes

These economical little tuna fish cakes are quick to make. Either use fresh mashed potatoes, or make a less fussy version with instant mashed potatoes.

INGREDIENTS 🍎

Serves 4

1¼ cups cooked mashed
   potatoes
7oz can tuna in vegetable oil,
   drained
¾ cup canned or frozen corn kernels
2 tbsp chopped fresh parsley
1 cup fresh white or whole wheat
   bread crumbs
salt and black pepper
lemon wedges, to serve

1 Place the mashed potato in a bowl and stir in the tuna, corn kernels, and chopped parsley.

2 Season to taste with salt and pepper, then shape into eight patty shapes with your hands.

3 Spread out the bread crumbs on a plate and press the fish cakes into the bread crumbs to coat lightly, then place on a baking sheet.

4 Cook the fish cakes under a moderately hot broiler until crisp and golden brown, turning once. Serve hot, with lemon wedges and fresh vegetables.

-------- VARIATIONS --------

For simple variations that are just as pleasing and nutritious, try using canned sardines, red or pink salmon, or smoked mackerel in place of the tuna.

-------- COOK'S TIP --------

To give the fish cakes a crisper crust, dip in beaten egg before coating them in the bread crumbs, then fry in a little hot oil until golden brown.

Seafood Salad Provençale

You can't beat this salad for an almost instant starter or main course, and it is perfect for a buffet table as it keeps so well.

INGREDIENTS

Serves 4

12oz mixed cooked seafood such as (shelled shrimp, mussels, clams, crabsticks)
2 tbsp ready-made tomato sauce
1 garlic clove, crushed
4 tbsp pimiento or mixed bell pepper antipasti
4 tbsp marinated artichokes
½ yellow bell pepper, seeded and sliced
lemon juice, to taste
2 tbsp white wine (optional)
salt and black pepper
2 tbsp chopped fresh parsley and whole shrimp, to garnish

1 Toss the seafood in the tomato sauce, add the garlic and leave for 5–10 minutes to absorb the flavors.

2 Mix together the pimiento or mixed bell pepper antipasti with the artichokes, the yellow bell pepper, lemon juice and wine, if using.

3 Stir in the seafood mixture, season to taste, and chill. Sprinkle with chopped parsley and garnish with whole shrimp before serving.

Monkfish and Potato Kabobs

Monkfish is a good, firm fish, so it works well on kabobs and when cooked over a fierce heat.

INGREDIENTS

Serves 4

12–16 small new potatoes, cooked
12–16 seedless grapes
4in piece cucumber, peeled and cut in eight pieces
10–12oz monkfish tail, boned and cubed
6 tbsp butter
grated rind and juice of 1 lime
1 tsp grated fresh ginger root
1 tbsp chopped fresh parsley
3–4 tbsp white wine
salt and black pepper

1 Arrange the potatoes, grapes, cucumber and monkfish cubes alternately on skewers.

2 Melt two-thirds of the butter and stir in the lime rind and juice, ginger, seasoning and half the parsley. Brush this all over the kabobs.

3 Preheat the broiler and cook the kabobs, in a dish or on a sheet of foil to catch all the juices, for 2 minutes on each side. Baste occasionally.

4 When cooked, transfer the kabobs to hot plates while heating the juices with the wine and the remaining butter. Check the seasoning, sprinkle the kabobs with parsley and serve with a salad and the tangy lime sauce.

Mackerel with Mustard and Lemon

Mackerel must be really fresh to be enjoyed. Look for bright, firm-looking fish.

INGREDIENTS

Serves 4
4 fresh mackerel, about 10oz each, gutted and cleaned
6–8oz young spinach leaves

For the mustard and lemon butter
½ cup butter, melted
2 tbsp whole grain mustard
grated rind of 1 lemon
2 tbsp lemon juice
3 tbsp chopped fresh parsley
salt and black pepper

1 To prepare each mackerel, cut off the heads just behind the gills, using a sharp knife, then cut along the belly so that the fish can be opened out flat.

2 Place the fish on a board, skin-side up, and, with the heel of your hand, press along the backbone to loosen it.

3 Turn the fish the right way up and pull the bone away from the flesh. Remove the tail and cut each fish in half lengthwise. Wash and pat dry.

4 Score the skin three or four times, then season the fish. To make the mustard and lemon butter, mix together the melted butter, mustard, lemon rind and juice, parsley and seasoning. Place the mackerel on a broiling rack. Brush a little of the butter over the mackerel and broil for 5 minutes each side, basting occasionally, until cooked through.

5 Arrange the spinach leaves in the center of four large plates. Place the mackerel on top. Heat the remaining butter in a small pan until sizzling and pour over the mackerel. Serve at once.

Mackerel Kabobs with Parsley Dressing

Oily fish such as mackerel are ideal for broiling as they cook quickly and need no extra oil.

INGREDIENTS

Serves 4
1lb mackerel fillets
finely grated rind and juice of
  1 lemon
3 tbsp chopped fresh parsley
12 cherry tomatoes
8 pitted ripe olives
salt and black pepper

1 Cut the fish into 1½in chunks and place in a bowl with half the lemon rind and juice, half of the parsley and some seasoning. Cover the bowl and leave to marinate for 30 minutes.

2 Thread the chunks of fish onto eight long wooden or metal skewers, alternating them with the cherry tomatoes and olives. Cook the kabobs under a hot broiler for 3–4 minutes, turning the kabobs occasionally, until the fish is cooked.

3 Mix the remaining lemon rind and juice with the remaining parsley in a small bowl, then season to taste with salt and pepper. Spoon the dressing over the kabobs and serve hot, with plain boiled rice or noodles and a leafy green salad.

COOK'S TIP

When using wooden or bamboo kabob skewers, soak them first in a bowl of cold water for a few minutes to help prevent them burning.

VARIATION

Other firm fleshed could be used in place of the mackerel – for a special occasion you could opt for salmon fillet or monkfish tail. Or try a mixture of the two, thread the fish chunks alternately on to the skewers with the tomatoes and olives.

Seafood Crêpes

The combination of fresh and smoked haddock imparts a wonderful flavor to the filling.

INGREDIENTS

Serves 4–6

For the crêpes
1 cup flour
pinch of salt
1 egg, plus 1 egg yolk
1¼ cups milk
1 tbsp melted butter, plus extra for
   cooking
2–3oz Gruyère cheese, grated

For the filling
8oz smoked haddock fillet
8oz fresh haddock fillet
1¼ cups milk
⅔ cup light cream
3 tbsp butter
4 tbsp flour
freshly grated nutmeg
2 hard-boiled eggs, shelled and
   chopped
salt and black pepper
curly salad leaves, to serve

1 To make the crêpes, sift the flour and salt into a bowl. Make a well in the center and add the eggs. Whisk the eggs, starting to incorporate some of the flour from around the edges.

2 Gradually add the milk, whisking all the time until the batter is smooth and the consistency of thin cream. Stir in the melted butter.

3 Heat a small crêpe pan or omelette pan until hot, then rub around the inside of the pan with a pad of paper towel dipped in melted butter.

4 Pour about 2 tbsp of the batter into the pan, then tip the pan to coat the base evenly. Cook for about 30 seconds until the underside of the crepe is brown.

5 Flip the crêpe over and cook the other side until lightly browned. Repeat to make 12 crêpes, rubbing the pan with melted butter between each crepe. Stack the crêpes as you make them between sheets of wax paper. Keep warm on a plate set over a pan of simmering water.

6 Put the haddock fillets in a large pan. Add the milk and poach for 6–8 minutes, until just tender. Lift out the fish using a slotted spoon and, when cool enough to handle, remove the skin and any bones. Reserve the milk.

7 Measure the light cream into a measuring cup, then strain enough of the milk into the cup to make the quantity up to 1⅞ cups.

8 Melt the butter in a pan, stir in the flour and cook gently for 1 minute. Gradually mix in the milk mixture, stirring continuously to make a smooth sauce. Cook for 2–3 minutes, until thickened. Season with salt, pepper and nutmeg. Coarsely flake the haddock and fold into the sauce with the eggs. Leave to cool.

9 Preheat the oven to 350°F. Divide the filling among the crêpes. Fold the sides of each crêpe into the center, then roll them up to enclose the filling completely.

10 Butter four or six individual ovenproof dishes and arrange 2–3 filled crêpes in each, or butter one large dish for all the crêpes. Brush with melted butter and cook for 15 minutes. Sprinkle over the Gruyère and cook for a further 5 minutes, until warmed through. Serve hot with a few curly salad leaves.

VARIATION

For a different taste, add cooked, peeled shrimp, smoked mussels or cooked fresh, shelled mussels to the filling, instead of the chopped hard-boiled eggs.

Stuffed Sole Rolls

Sole fillets are a good choice because they are mild in flavor, easy to cook, and free of bones. Have your fillets prepared when you buy them.

INGREDIENTS 🍎

Serves 4

2 medium carrots, grated
1 medium zucchini, grated
4 tbsp fresh whole wheat bread crumbs
1 tbsp lime or lemon juice
4 sole fillets
salt and black pepper

1 Preheat the oven to 400°F. Mix together the grated carrots and zucchini. Stir in the bread crumbs, lime juice, and seasoning to taste.

2 Lay the fish fillets skin side up and divide the stuffing between them, spreading it evenly.

3 Roll up to enclose the stuffing and place in an ovenproof dish. Cover the dish and bake for about 30 minutes, or until the fish flakes easily. Serve hot with new potatoes.

— COOK'S TIP —

This recipe creates its own delicious juices, but for an extra sauce, stir chopped fresh parsley into a little low fat fromage frais and serve with the fish.

— VARIATION —

For a change, buy thick pieces of cod or salmon fillet and simply top them with the carrot and zucchini mixture.

Haddock with Parsley Sauce

As the fish has to be kept warm while the sauce is made, take care not to overcook it.

INGREDIENTS

Serves 4

4 haddock fillets, about 6oz each
4 tbsp butter
⅔ cup milk
⅔ cup fish stock
1 bay leaf
4 tsp flour
4 tbsp cream
1 egg yolk
3 tbsp chopped fresh parsley
grated rind and juice of ½ lemon
salt and black pepper

1 Place the fish in a frying pan, add half the butter, the milk, fish stock, bay leaf and seasoning, and heat over low-medium heat to simmering point. Lower the heat, cover the pan and poach the fish for 10–15 minutes, depending on the thickness of the fillets, until the fish is tender and the flesh just begins to flake.

2 Transfer the fish to a warmed serving plate, cover the fish and keep warm while you make the sauce. Return the cooking liquid to the heat and bring to a boil, stirring. Simmer for about 4 minutes, then remove from the heat.

3 Melt the remaining butter in a saucepan, stir in the flour and cook, stirring, for 1 minute. Remove from the heat and gradually stir in the fish cooking liquid. Return to the heat and bring to a boil, stirring. Simmer for about 4 minutes, stirring frequently. Discard the bay leaf.

4 Remove the pan from the heat, blend the cream into the egg yolk, then stir into the sauce with the parsley. Reheat gently, stirring, for a few minutes; do not allow to boil.

5 Remove from the heat and add the lemon juice and rind, and season to taste. Pour into a warmed sauceboat and serve with the fish.

MID-WEEK SUPPERS

In the middle of the week, when you are short of time to cook, dishes made with fish or seafood are ideal – Baked Fish Creole-Style can be put together very speedily. If you have more time, fish pies, either topped with potato or filo pastry, are good. If you would like to try something a little different, opt for Moroccan Fish Tagine, Cod with Spiced Red Lentils or Spanish Seafood Paella.

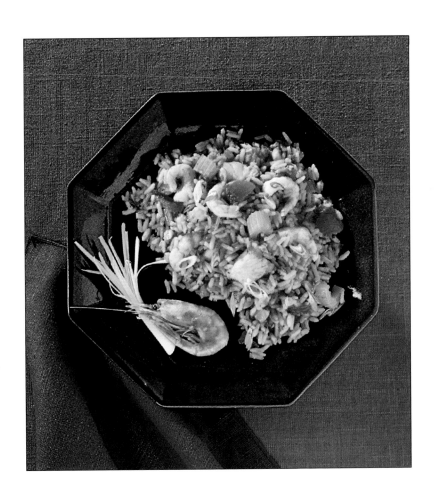

Fisherman's Casserole

INGREDIENTS

Serves 4–6

1lb mixed firm fish fillets such as cod,
    haddock and monkfish
4 tbsp butter
1 onion, sliced
1 celery stick, sliced
12oz potatoes, cut into chunks
3⅔ cups fish stock
bouquet garni
5oz frozen fava beans
1¼ cups milk
4oz cooked, peeled shrimp
8 shelled mussels
salt and black pepper
chopped parsley, to garnish

1 Skin the fish and cut the flesh into bite-sized chunks using a large sharp knife. Heat the butter in a saucepan, then fry the onion and celery until softened but not coloured. Stir the chunks of potato into the pan and cook for 1–2 minutes.

2 Add the stock and bouquet garni. Bring to the boil, cover and simmer for 20 minutes, until tender.

3 Add the fish, beans and milk and simmer for 6 minutes, until the fish flakes. Add the shrimp, mussels and seasoning and warm through. Sprinkle with parsley to serve.

Potato-topped Fish Pie

INGREDIENTS

Serves 4

1¾ cups milk
1 bay leaf
¼ onion, sliced
1lb haddock or cod fillet
8oz smoked haddock fillet
3 hard-boiled eggs, chopped
5 tbsp butter
2 tbsp flour
1 cup peas
3oz shrimp (optional)
2 tbsp chopped fresh parsley
lemon juice, to taste
1¼lb cooked mashed potatoes
4 tbsp hot milk
4 tbsp grated Cheddar cheese
salt and black pepper

1 Place 1½ cups milk, the bay leaf and onion in a saucepan, then add the fish. Cover and poach for 8–10 minutes. Strain and reserve the milk. Flake the fish into a pie dish, discarding the skin and any bones. Add the eggs.

2 Melt 2 tbsp of the butter in a saucepan, stir in the flour and cook gently for 1 minute, stirring. Remove from the heat and stir in the reserved milk. Return to the heat and bring to the boil, stirring. Simmer the sauce for 4 minutes, stirring all the time. Remove from the heat and stir in the peas and shrimp.

3 Add the parsley, lemon juice and seasoning to taste. Pour the sauce over the fish and eggs and carefully mix together.

4 Preheat the oven to 350°F. Gently heat the remaining butter in the remaining milk in a small saucepan, then beat into the potato. Spoon the potato mixture evenly over the fish and fork up the surface.

5 Sprinkle the cheese over the pie, then bake for 25–30 minutes, until golden. Serve hot.

Smoked Trout Pilaf

Smoked trout might seem an unusual partner for rice, but this is a winning combination.

INGREDIENTS

Serves 4

1¼ cups white basmati rice
3 tbsp butter
2 onions, sliced into rings
1 garlic clove, crushed
2 bay leaves
2 whole cloves
2 green cardamom pods
2 cinnamon sticks
1 tsp cumin seeds
4 smoked trout fillets, skinned
½ cup slivered almonds, toasted
⅓ cup seedless raisins
2 tbsp chopped fresh parsley
mango chutney and poppadoms, to serve

1 Wash the rice thoroughly in several changes of water and drain well. Set aside. Melt the butter in a large frying pan and fry the onions until well browned, stirring frequently.

2 Add the garlic, bay leaves, cloves, cardamom pods, cinnamon and cumin seeds and stir-fry for 1 minute.

3 Stir in the rice, then add 2½ cups boiling water. Bring to a boil. Cover the pan tightly, reduce the heat and cook very gently for 20–25 minutes, until the water has been absorbed and the rice is tender.

4 Flake the smoked trout and add to the pan with the almonds and raisins. Fork through gently. Re-cover the pan and allow the smoked trout to warm in the rice for a few minutes. Scatter over the parsley and serve with mango chutney and poppadoms.

Cod with Spiced Red Lentils

INGREDIENTS

Serves 4

1 cup red lentils
¼ tsp ground turmeric
2½ cups fish stock
2 tbsp vegetable oil
1½ tsp cumin seeds
1 tbsp grated fresh ginger root
½ tsp cayenne pepper
1 tbsp lemon juice
2 tbsp chopped fresh coriander
1lb cod fillets, skinned and cut into
  large chunks
salt, to taste
coriander leaves and lemon wedges,
  to garnish

1 Put the lentils in a pan with the turmeric and stock. Bring to a boil, cover and simmer for 20–25 minutes, until the lentils are just tender. Remove from the heat and add salt.

2 Heat the oil in a small frying pan. Add the cumin seeds and, when they begin to pop, add the ginger and cayenne pepper. Stir-fry the spices for a few seconds, then pour on to the lentils. Add the lemon juice and the coriander and stir in gently.

3 Lay the pieces of cod on top of the lentils, cover the pan and then cook gently over a low heat for about 10–15 minutes, until the fish is tender.

4 Transfer the lentils and cod to warmed serving plates. Sprinkle over the coriander leaves and garnish each serving with one or two lemon wedges. Serve hot.

Herrings in Oatmeal with Mustard

INGREDIENTS

Serves 4

about 1 tbsp Dijon-style mustard
about 1½ tsp tarragon vinegar
¾ cup thick mayonnaise
4 herrings, about 8oz each
1 lemon, halved
¾ cup medium oatmeal
salt and black pepper

1 Beat mustard and vinegar to taste into the mayonnaise. Chill lightly.

2 Place one fish at a time on a board, cut side down and opened out. Press gently along the backbone with your thumbs. Turn over the fish and carefully lift away the backbone.

3 Squeeze lemon juice over both sides of the fish, then season with salt and pepper. Fold the fish in half, skin side outwards.

4 Preheat a broiler until fairly hot. Place the oatmeal on a plate, then coat each herring evenly in the oatmeal, pressing it in gently.

5 Place the herrings on a broiler rack and broil the fish for 3–4 minutes on each side, until the skin is golden brown and crisp and the flesh flakes easily. Serve hot with the mustard sauce, served separately.

Fish and Fries

INGREDIENTS

Serves 4

1 cup self-rising flour
⅔ cup water
1½lb potatoes
1½lb piece skinned cod fillet, cut into four pieces
oil, for deep frying
salt and black pepper
lemon wedges, to serve

1 Stir the flour and salt together in a bowl, then form a well in the center. Gradually pour in the water, whisking in the flour to make a smooth batter. Leave for 30 minutes.

2 Cut the potatoes into strips about ½in wide and 2in long, using a sharp knife. Place the potatoes in a colander and rinse them in cold water, then drain and dry well.

3 Heat the oil in a deep-fat fryer or large heavy pan to 300°F. Using the wire basket, lower the potatoes in batches into the oil and cook for 5–6 minutes, shaking the basket occasionally until the potatoes are soft but not browned. Remove the fries from the oil and drain thoroughly on paper towels.

4 Heat the oil in the deep-fat fryer to 375°F. Season the fish. Stir the batter, then dip the pieces of fish in turn into it, allowing the excess to drain off.

5 Working in two batches if necessary, lower the fish into the oil and fry for 6–8 minutes, until crisp and brown. Drain the fish on paper towels and keep warm.

6 Add the fries in batches to the oil and cook for 2–3 minutes, until brown and crisp. Keep hot. Sprinkle with salt and serve with the fish, accompanied by lemon wedges.

Smoked Haddock Lyonnaise

INGREDIENTS

Serves 4

1lb smoked haddock
⅔ cup milk
2 onions, chopped
1 tbsp butter
1 tbsp cornstarch
⅔ cup Greek-style yogurt
1 tsp ground turmeric
1 tsp paprika
4oz mushrooms, sliced
2 celery stalks, chopped
12oz firm cooked potatoes, preferably
   cold, diced
2 tbsp olive oil
½–1 cup soft white bread crumbs
salt and black pepper

1 Poach the fish in the milk until just cooked. Remove the fish, reserving the liquid, then flake the fish and discard the skin and bones. Set aside.

2 Fry half the chopped onion in the butter until translucent. Stir in the cornstarch, then gradually blend in the fish cooking liquid and the yogurt and cook until thickened and smooth.

3 Stir in the turmeric, paprika, mushrooms and celery. Season to taste and add the flaked fish. Spoon into an ovenproof dish. Preheat the oven to 375°F.

4 Fry the remaining onion in the oil until translucent. Add the diced potatoes and stir until lightly coated in oil. Sprinkle on the bread crumbs and seasoning.

5 Spoon this mixture over the fish and bake for 20–30 minutes, or until the top is nicely crisp and golden.

COOK'S TIP

Chopped cooked parsnips or turnips could also be used for the topping, but as with the potato, it is better if they are firm.

Golden Fish and Shrimp Pie

INGREDIENTS

Serves 4–6

1½lb white fish fillets
1¼ cups milk
flavoring ingredients (onion slices,
    bay leaf and black peppercorns)
4oz cooked, peeled shrimp, defrosted
    if frozen
½ cup butter
½ cup flour
1¼ cups light cream
3oz Gruyère cheese, grated
1 bunch watercress, leaves only, chopped
1 tsp Dijon mustard
5 sheets filo pastry
salt and black pepper

1 Place the fish fillets in a pan, pour over the milk and add the flavoring ingredients. Bring just to a boil, then cover and simmer for 10–12 minutes, until the fish is almost tender.

2 Skin and bone the fish, then roughly flake into a shallow oven-proof dish. Scatter the shrimp over the fish. Strain the milk and reserve.

3 Melt 4 tbsp of the butter in a pan. Stir in the flour and cook for 1 minute. Stir in the reserved milk and cream. Bring to a boil, stirring, then simmer for 2–3 minutes, until the sauce has thickened.

4 Remove the pan from the heat and stir in the Gruyère, watercress, mustard and seasoning to taste. Pour over the fish and leave to cool.

5 Preheat the oven to 375°F. Melt the remaining butter. Brush one sheet of filo pastry with a little butter, then crumple up loosely and place on top of the filling. Repeat this procedure with the remaining filo sheets and butter until they are all used up and the pie is completely covered.

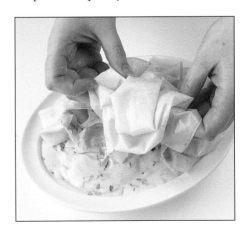

6 Bake in the oven for 25–30 minutes, until the pastry is golden and crisp.

Herrings with Red Salsa

Herrings are one of the most economical and nutritious fish. If you buy them ready filleted, they're much easier to eat than the whole fish.

INGREDIENTS

Serves 4
2 tbsp skim milk
2 tsp Dijon-style mustard
2 large herrings, filleted
⅔ cup oatmeal
salt and black pepper

For the salsa
1 small red bell pepper, seeded
4 medium tomatoes
1 scallion, chopped
1 tbsp lime juice
1 tsp sugar

1 Preheat the oven to 400°F. To make the salsa, place the pepper, tomatoes, scallion, lime juice, sugar, and seasoning in a food processor. Process until finely chopped.

2 Mix the milk and mustard, and the oatmeal, and pepper. Dip fillets into the milk mixture, then oatmeal to coat.

3 Place on a baking sheet, then bake for 20 minutes. Serve with the salsa.

— VARIATION —

If herring fillets are unavailable, then make this recipe with mackerel fillets – they would be equally delicious with the pepper and tomato salsa.

Spiced Rainbow Trout

Farmed rainbow trout are very good value and cook very quickly under a broiler or on a barbecue. Herring and mackerel can be cooked in this way too.

INGREDIENTS

Serves 4
4 large rainbow trout fillets (about 5oz each)
1 tbsp ground coriander
1 garlic clove, crushed
2 tbsp finely chopped fresh mint
1 tsp paprika
¾ cup plain yogurt
salad and pita bread, to serve

1 With a sharp knife, slash the flesh of the fish fillets through the skin fairly deeply at intervals.

2 Mix together the coriander, garlic, mint, paprika, and yogurt. Spread this mixture evenly over the fish and leave to marinate for about 1 hour.

3 Cook the fish under a moderately hot broiler or on a barbecue, turning occasionally, until crisp and golden. Serve hot, with a crisp salad and some warmed pita bread.

— COOK'S TIP —

If you are using the broiler, it is best to line the pan with foil before cooking the trout.

— VARIATION —

The flavorful spicy mixture can be used for other fish fillets, such as haddock or cod. Or, you could use the mixture for fish kabobs. Coat chunks or strips of fish, then thread on to skewers.

Spanish Seafood Paella

Ingredients

Serves 4

4 tbsp olive oil
8oz monkfish or cod, skinned and cut
   into chunks
3 cleaned baby squid, body cut into
   rings and tentacles chopped
1 red mullet, filleted, skinned and cut
   into chunks (optional)
1 onion, chopped
3 garlic cloves, finely chopped
1 red bell pepper, seeded and sliced
4 tomatoes, skinned and chopped
1¼ cups arborio rice
1⅞ cups fish stock
⅔ cup white wine
¾ cup frozen peas
4–5 saffron strands soaked in 2 tbsp hot
   water
1 cup cooked, peeled shrimp
8 fresh mussels in shells, scrubbed
salt and black pepper
1 tbsp chopped fresh parsley, to garnish
lemon wedges, to serve

1 Heat 2 tbsp of the oil in a large frying pan and add the monkfish or cod, the squid and the red mullet, if using, to the pan. Stir-fry for 2 minutes, then transfer the fish to a bowl with all the juices and reserve.

2 Heat the remaining 2 tbsp of oil in the pan and add the onion, garlic and pepper. Fry for 6–7 minutes, stirring frequently, until the onion and pepper have softened.

3 Stir in the tomatoes and fry for 2 minutes, then add the rice, stirring to coat the grains with oil, and cook for 2–3 minutes. Pour on the fish stock and wine and add the peas, saffron and water. Season well and mix.

4 Gently stir in the reserved cooked fish with all the juices, followed by the shrimp; and then push the mussels into the rice. Cover and cook over a gentle heat for about 30 minutes, or until the stock has been absorbed but the mixture is still moist.

5 Remove from the heat, keep covered and leave to stand for 5 minutes. Sprinkle with parsley and serve with lemon wedges.

Fish Jambalaya

Jambalaya, from New Orleans, is not unlike a paella, but much more spicy. The name comes from the French word jambon, and tells us that the dish is based on ham, but you can add other ingredients of your choice, including all sorts of fish and shellfish.

INGREDIENTS

Serves 4

2 tbsp oil
4oz smoked bacon, rinds removed, diced
1 onion, chopped
2 stalks celery, chopped
2 large garlic cloves, chopped
1 tsp cayenne pepper
2 bay leaves
1 tsp dried oregano
½ tsp dried thyme
4 tomatoes, peeled and chopped
⅔ cup ready-made tomato sauce
1¾ cups long grain rice
2 cups fish stock
6oz firm white fish (such as halibut, cod, scrod or haddock), skinned, boned and cubed
1 cup cooked, peeled shrimp
salt and black pepper
2 chopped scallions, to garnish

1 Heat the oil in a large saucepan and fry the bacon until crisp. Add the onion and celery and stir until beginning to stick on the base of the pan.

2 Add the garlic, cayenne pepper, herbs, tomatoes and seasoning and mix well. Stir in the tomato sauce, rice and stock and bring to the boil.

3 Preheat the oven to 350°F. Gently stir in the fish and transfer to an ovenproof dish. Cover tightly with foil and bake for 20–30 minutes, until the rice is just tender. Stir in the shrimp and heat through. Serve sprinkled with the scallions.

COOK'S TIP

A traditional and easy way to serve jambalaya is to fill an 8oz cup with the mixture and unmold it onto a hot plate. Then serve with Creole sauce (which you can buy ready-made) and garnish each portion with a whole shrimp.

Seafood Pilaf

This all-in-one-pan main course is a satisfying meal for any day of the week. For a special meal, you could substitute dry white wine for the orange juice.

INGREDIENTS 🍎

Serves 4
2 tsp olive oil
1¼ cups long grain rice
1 tsp ground turmeric
1 red bell pepper, seeded and diced
1 small onion, finely chopped
2 medium zucchini, sliced
2 cups button mushrooms, halved
1½ cups fish or chicken stock
⅔ cup orange juice
12oz white fish fillets
12 fresh mussels in the shell (or cooked, shelled mussels)
salt and ground black pepper
grated rind of 1 orange, to garnish

1 Heat the oil in a large, nonstick pan and sauté the rice and turmeric over low heat for about 1 minute.

2 Add the pepper, onion, zucchini, and mushrooms. Stir in the broth and orange juice. Bring to a boil.

3 Reduce the heat and add the fish. Cover and simmer gently for about 15 minutes, until the rice is tender and the liquid absorbed. Stir in the mussels and heat thoroughly. Adjust the seasoning, sprinkle with orange rind, and serve hot.

— VARIATION —

If you prefer, use fresh mussels in the shell. Scrub them well and discard any that remain open. Add to the rice about 5 minutes before the end of cooking.

Salmon Pasta with Parsley Sauce

INGREDIENTS 🍎

Serves 4
1lb salmon fillet, skinned
3 cups pasta, such as penne or twists
6oz cherry tomatoes, halved
⅔ cup low fat crème fraîche
3 tbsp finely chopped parsley
finely grated rind of ½ orange
salt and black pepper

— COOK'S TIP —

If you can't find low fat crème fraîche, then use ordinary sour cream or heavy cream instead.

1 Cut the salmon into bite-sized pieces, arrange on a heatproof plate, and cover with foil.

2 Bring a large pan of salted water to the boil, add the pasta, and return to a boil. Place the plate of salmon on top and simmer for 10–12 minutes, until the pasta and salmon are cooked.

3 Drain the pasta and toss with the tomatoes and salmon. Mix together the crème fraîche, parsley, orange rind, and pepper to taste, then toss into the salmon and pasta and serve hot or cold.

Baked Fish Creole-style

INGREDIENTS

Serves 4

1 tbsp vegetable oil
2 tbsp butter
1 onion, thinly sliced
1 garlic clove, chopped
1 red bell pepper, seeded, halved
   and sliced
1 green bell pepper, seeded, halved
   and sliced
14oz can chopped tomatoes with basil
1 tbsp tomato paste
2 tbsp chopped capers
3–4 drops Tabasco sauce
4 tail end pieces cod or haddock fillets
   (about 6oz each), skinned
6 basil leaves, shredded
3 tbsp fresh bread crumbs
¼ cup grated Cheddar cheese
2 tsp chopped fresh parsley
salt and black pepper
fresh basil sprigs, to garnish

1 Preheat the oven to 450°F. Grease an ovenproof dish.

2 Heat the oil and half the butter in a pan and add the onion. Fry for about 6–7 minutes, until softened, then add the garlic, peppers, chopped tomatoes, tomato paste, capers and Tabasco and season well. Cover and cook for 15 minutes, then uncover and simmer gently for 5 minutes to reduce slightly.

3 Place the fish fillets in the ovenproof dish, dot with the remaining 1 tbsp butter and season lightly. Spoon over the tomato and pepper sauce and sprinkle over the shredded basil. Bake in the oven for about 10 minutes.

4 Meanwhile, mix together the bread crumbs, cheese and parsley in a bowl.

5 Remove the fish from the oven and scatter the cheese and bread crumbs over the top. Return to the oven and bake for a further 10 minutes, until lightly browned.

6 Let the fish stand for about a minute, then, using a spatula, carefully transfer each topped fillet to warmed plates. Garnish with sprigs of fresh basil and serve hot.

Moroccan Fish Tagine

Tagine is actually the name of the large Moroccan cooking pot used for this type of cooking, but you can of course use an ordinary casserole instead.

INGREDIENTS 🍎

Serves 4

2 garlic cloves, crushed
2 tbsp ground cumin
2 tbsp paprika
1 small red fresh chili (optional)
2 tbsp tomato paste
4 tbsp lemon juice
4 whiting or cod steaks, about
  6oz each
12oz tomatoes, sliced
2 green bell peppers, seeded and
  thinly sliced
salt and black pepper
chopped fresh coriander, to garnish

1 Mix together the garlic, cumin, paprika, chili, tomato paste and lemon juice. Spread this mixture over the fish, then cover and chill for about 30 minutes to let the flavor penetrate.

2 Preheat the oven to 400°F. Arrange half of the sliced tomatoes and peppers in a baking dish.

3 Cover with the fish, in one layer, then arrange the remaining sliced tomatoes and pepper on top. Cover the baking dish with foil and bake for about 45 minutes, until the fish is cooked through. Sprinkle with chopped coriander and serve.

—— COOK'S TIP ——

If you are preparing this dish for a dinner party, it can be assembled completely and stored in the fridge, ready for baking when needed.

—— VARIATION ——

For a colorful variation, replace one of the green peppers with a yellow or orange pepper. You could also use chopped parsley, if you can't find fresh coriander.

Crunchy-topped Cod

Delicious and quick to cook, this is ideal for weekday meals.

INGREDIENTS

Serves 4
4 pieces cod fillet, about 4oz each,
   skinned
2 medium tomatoes, sliced
1 cup fresh whole wheat bread crumbs
2 tbsp chopped fresh parsley
finely grated rind and juice of ½ lemon
1 tsp sunflower oil
salt and black pepper

1 Preheat the oven to 400°F. Arrange the cod fillets in a wide, shallow ovenproof dish.

2 Arrange the tomato slices on top. Mix together the bread crumbs, fresh parsley, lemon rind and juice, and the oil with seasoning to taste.

3 Spoon the crumb mixture evenly over the fish, then bake for 15–20 minutes. Serve hot.

VARIATION

Choose firm, ripe tomatoes with plenty of flavor. In the summer you may be lucky enough to find fresh plum tomatoes, which are perfect for this tasty dish.

Crumbly Fish Bake

This fish pie is colorful, healthy, and best of all very easy to make. For a more economical version, omit the shrimp and replace with more fish fillet.

INGREDIENTS

Serves 4
12oz haddock fillet, skinned
2 tbsp cornstarch
4oz cooked, peeled shrimp
7oz can corn kernels, drained
¾ cup frozen peas
⅔ cup skim milk
⅔ cup low fat fromage frais
1½ cups fresh whole wheat bread
   crumbs
½ cup shredded low fat Cheddar cheese
salt and black pepper

1 Preheat the oven to 375°F. Cut the haddock into bite-sized pieces and toss in cornstarch.

2 Place the fish, shrimp, corn, and peas in an ovenproof dish. Beat together the milk, fromage frais, and seasonings, then pour into the dish.

3 Mix together the bread crumbs and shredded cheese, then spoon evenly over the top. Bake for 25–30 minutes, or until golden brown. Serve hot, with fresh vegetables.

VARIATION

This quick recipe can be prepared well ahead and chilled – keep the bread crumb topping separately, then sprinkle over the fish mixture just before baking.

Cod Creole

INGREDIENTS

Serves 4

1lb cod fillets, skinned
1 tbsp lime or lemon juice
2 tsp olive oil
1 medium onion, finely chopped
1 green bell pepper, seeded and sliced
½ tsp cayenne pepper
½ tsp garlic salt
14oz can chopped tomatoes

COOK'S TIP

Be careful not to overcook the fish – or to let it bubble too fast in the sauce – as the chunks will break up.

1 Cut the cod fillets into bite-sized chunks and sprinkle with the lime or lemon juice.

2 In a large, non-stick pan, heat the olive oil and sauté the onion and pepper gently until softened. Add the cayenne pepper and garlic salt.

3 Stir in the cod with the chopped tomatoes. Bring to a boil, then cover and simmer for about 5 minutes, or until the fish flakes easily. Serve with boiled rice or potatoes.

Five-spice Fish

Chinese mixtures of spicy, sweet, and sour flavors are particularly successful with fish – and dinner is ready in minutes!

INGREDIENTS

Serves 4

4 white fish fillets, such as cod, haddock
  or flounder (about 6oz each)
1 tsp Chinese five-spice powder
4 tsp cornstarch
1 tbsp sesame or sunflower oil
3 scallions, shredded
1 tsp finely chopped fresh ginger root
5oz button mushrooms, sliced
4oz baby corn, sliced
2 tbsp soy sauce
3 tbsp dry sherry or apple juice
1 tsp sugar
salt and black pepper

1 Toss the fish in the five-spice powder and cornstarch to coat.

2 Heat the oil in a frying pan or wok and stir-fry the scallions, ginger, mushrooms, and corn for about 1 minute. Add the fish and cook for 2–3 minutes, turning once.

3 Mix together the soy sauce, sherry, and sugar, then pour over the fish. Simmer for 2 minutes, adjust the seasoning, then serve with noodles and stir-fried vegetables.

COOK'S TIP

Chinese noodle are available in most large supermarkets and make a very speedy accompaniment since they are just soaked in boiling water for a few minutes.

DINNER PARTY DISHES

The perfect food for entertaining is easy to prepare and serve, yet looks
fabulous and tastes wonderful. Fish makes an especially good choice for
a main course, as it is not too rich, yet is full of flavor. If you prefer to
have the main dish prepared ahead of time try Monkfish Brochettes.
However, if you don't mind cooking at the last minute, then Tuna
with Pan-fried Tomatoes or seared salmon are perfect choices.

Halibut with Fennel and Orange

INGREDIENTS

Serves 4

1 fennel bulb, thinly sliced
grated rind and juice of 1 orange
⅔ cup dry white wine
4 halibut steaks, about 7oz each
4 tbsp butter
salt and black pepper
fennel fronds, to garnish

1 Preheat the oven to 350°F. Butter a shallow baking dish.

2 Add the fennel to a saucepan of boiling water, return to a boil and boil for 4–6 minutes, until just tender.

3 Meanwhile, cook the orange rind, juice and wine until reduced by half.

4 Drain the fennel well, then spread in the baking dish and season. Arrange the halibut on the fennel, season, dot with butter, then pour over the reduced orange and wine.

5 Cover and bake for about 20 minutes, until the flesh flakes. Serve garnished with fennel fronds.

Salmon with Cucumber Sauce

INGREDIENTS

Serves 6–8

4lb salmon, gutted
  and scaled
melted butter, for brushing
3 parsley or thyme sprigs
½ lemon, halved
1 large cucumber, peeled
2 tbsp butter
½ cup dry white wine
3 tbsp finely chopped fresh dill
4 tbsp sour cream
salt and black pepper

1 Preheat the oven to 425°F. Season the salmon and brush inside and out with melted butter. Place the herbs and lemon in the cavity.

2 Wrap the salmon in foil, folding the edges together securely, then bake for 15 minutes. Remove the fish from the oven and leave in the foil for 1 hour, then remove the skin from the salmon.

3 Meanwhile, halve the cucumber lengthways, scoop out the seeds, then dice the flesh.

4 Place the cucumber in a strainer, toss lightly with salt, leave for about 30 minutes to drain, then rinse well and pat dry.

5 Heat the butter in a small saucepan, add the cucumber and cook for about 2 minutes, until translucent but not soft. Add the wine to the pan and boil briskly until the cucumber is dry.

6 Stir the chopped dill and sour cream into the cooked cucumber. Season to taste and serve immediately with the salmon.

Mediterranean Sole Rolls

Sun-dried tomatoes, pine nuts and anchovies make a really flavorful combination for the stuffing mixture.

INGREDIENTS

Serves 4

4 sole fillets, about 8oz each, skinned
6 tbsp butter
1 small onion, chopped
1 celery stalk, finely chopped
2 cups fresh white bread crumbs
3 tbsp chopped fresh parsley
2 tbsp pine nuts, toasted
3–4 pieces sun-dried tomatoes in oil, drained and chopped
2oz can anchovy fillets, drained and chopped
5 tbsp fish stock
black pepper

1 Preheat the oven to 350°F. Using a sharp knife, carefully cut the sole fillets in half lengthwise to make eight smaller fillets.

2 Melt the butter in a pan and add the onion and celery. Cover and cook over a low heat for about 15 minutes until softened. Do not allow to brown.

3 Mix together the bread crumbs, parsley, pine nuts, sun-dried tomatoes and anchovies. Stir in the softened vegetables with the buttery juices and season with pepper.

4 Divide the stuffing into eight portions. Taking one portion at a time, form the stuffing into balls, then roll up each one inside a sole fillet. Secure each roll with a toothpick.

5 Place the rolled-up fillets in a buttered ovenproof dish. Pour in the stock and cover the dish with buttered foil. Bake for about 20 minutes, or until the fish flakes easily. Remove the toothpicks, then serve with a little of the cooking juices drizzled over.

Red Mullet with Fennel

Other red-skinned fish, such as snapper, are also excellent cooked in this way – you'll need only two fish if they are large.

INGREDIENTS

Serves 4

3 small fennel bulbs
4 tbsp olive oil
2 small onions, thinly sliced
2–4 basil leaves
4 small or 2 large red snapper, cleaned
grated rind of ½ lemon
⅔ cup fish stock
4 tbsp butter
juice of 1 lemon

1 Snip off the feathery fronds from the fennel, finely chop and reserve for the garnish. Cut the fennel into wedges, leaving the layers attached at the root ends so the pieces stay intact.

2 Heat the oil in a frying pan large enough to take the fish in a single layer. Add the wedges of fennel and the onions and cook for 10–15 minutes, until softened and lightly browned.

3 Tuck a basil leaf inside each fish, then place on top of the vegetables. Sprinkle over the lemon rind. Pour in the stock and bring just to a boil. Cover and cook gently for 15–20 minutes, until the fish is tender.

4 Melt the butter in a small pan and, when it starts to sizzle and color slightly, add the lemon juice. Pour over the snapper, sprinkle with the reserved fennel fronds and serve.

Baked Trout with Olives

INGREDIENTS

Serves 4

1 cup fresh whole wheat
  bread crumbs
1oz chopped ham
½ cup finely chopped black olives
1 garlic clove, crushed
1 egg yolk
4 trout (about 6oz each)
½ cup dry vermouth
2 tbsp butter
1 tbsp flour
⅔ cup fish stock
3–4 tbsp light cream
salt and black pepper

1 Preheat the oven to 350°F. Mix the breadcrumbs, ham, olives, garlic, egg yolk and seasoning together. Pack into the trout cavities and place each one on a sheet of greased foil.

2 Pour 1 tbsp dry vermouth over each one, dot with half of the butter and wrap up closely. Bake for about 20–25 minutes, or until tender.

3 Melt the remaining butter in a small pan and blend in the flour. Whisk in the remaining vermouth, the stock and the juices which have come out of the fish during cooking and cook for 1–2 minutes until thickened.

4 Stir in the cream, then season the sauce to taste and pour a little over each fish before serving hot.

Salmon Cakes with Butter Sauce

Salmon fish cakes make a real treat for an informal dinner party. You could use any small tail pieces which are on sale.

INGREDIENTS

Makes 6

8oz tail piece of salmon, cooked
2 tbsp chopped fresh parsley
2 scallions, trimmed and chopped
grated rind and juice of ½ lemon
8oz cooked mashed potato (not too soft)
1 egg, beaten
1 cup fresh white bread crumbs
6 tbsp butter
salt and black pepper

1 Remove all the skin and bones from the fish and mash well. Add the parsley, scallions and 1 tsp of lemon rind and season with salt and black pepper.

2 Gently work in the potato and then shape into six rounds, triangles or croquettes. Chill for 20 minutes.

3 Coat well in egg and then the bread crumbs. Broil gently for 5 minutes each side, or until golden, or fry in a little butter and oil.

4 To make the butter sauce, melt the butter, whisk in the remaining lemon rind, the lemon juice, 1–2 tbsp water and seasoning to taste. Simmer for a few minutes and serve with the hot fish cakes.

Cod with Caper Sauce

The quick and easy sauce with a slightly sharp and 'nutty' flavour is a very effective way of enhancing this simple fish.

INGREDIENTS

Serves 4

4 cod steaks, about 6oz each
½ cup butter
1 tbsp vinegar from the caper jar
1 tbsp small capers
1 tbsp chopped fresh parsley
salt and black pepper
tarragon sprigs, to garnish

1 Preheat the broiler. Season the cod. Melt 2 tbsp of the butter, then brush some over one side of each piece of cod.

2 Broil the cod steaks for about 6 minutes, turn the fish over, brush with melted butter and cook for a further 5–6 minutes, or until the fish flakes easily.

3 Meanwhile, heat the remaining butter until it turns golden brown, then add the vinegar followed by the capers and stir well.

4 Pour the vinegar, butter and capers over the fish, sprinkle with parsley and garnish with the tarragon sprigs.

COOK'S TIP

Thick tail fillets of cod or haddock could be used in place of the cod steaks.

Trout with Hazelnuts

The chopped hazelnuts in this recipe make an interesting change from the flaked almonds normally used with trout.

INGREDIENTS

Serves 4
⅓ cup shelled hazelnuts, chopped
5 tbsp butter
4 trout, about 10oz each
2 tbsp lemon juice
salt and black pepper
lemon slices and flat leaf parsley sprigs,
   to serve

1 Preheat the broiler. Toast the hazelnuts in a single layer, stirring frequently, until the skins split. Then tip them on to a clean cloth and rub to remove the skins. Leave the nuts to cool, then chop them coarsely.

2 Heat 4 tbsp of the butter in a large frying pan. Season the trout inside and out, then fry two at a time for 12–15 minutes, turning once, until the trout are brown and the flesh flakes easily when tested with the point of a sharp knife.

MICROWAVE NOTE

You can use a microwave to prepare the nuts, spread them in a shallow dish and cook on full power until the skins split.

3 Drain the cooked trout on kitchen paper, then transfer to a warm serving plate and keep warm while frying the remaining trout in the same way. (If your frying pan is large enough, you could, of course, cook the trout in one batch.)

4 Add the remaining butter to the frying pan, then add the hazelnuts and fry them until evenly browned. Stir the lemon juice into the pan and mix well, then quickly pour the buttery sauce over the trout and serve at once, garnished with slices of lemon and flat leaf parsley sprigs.

Sole and Pesto Parcels

Serve the parcels hot from the oven to the table – the wax paper bakes translucent and looks attractive.

INGREDIENTS

Serves 4
6 tbsp butter
4 tsp pesto sauce
8 small sole fillets
1 small fennel bulb, cut into
  matchsticks
2 small carrots, cut into matchsticks
2 zucchini, cut into matchsticks
2 tsp finely grated lemon rind
salt and black pepper
basil leaves, to garnish

1 Preheat the oven to 375°F. Beat 4 tbsp of the butter with the pesto sauce and seasoning to taste. Skin the sole fillets, then spread the pesto butter over the skinned side of each and carefully roll up, starting from the thick end. Set the rolls on one aside.

2 Melt the remaining butter in a pan, add the fennel and carrots and sauté for 3 minutes. Add the zucchini and cook for 2 minutes. Remove from the heat. Add the lemon rind and seasoning.

3 Cut four squares of wax paper, each large enough to enclose two fish rolls. Brush with oil. Spoon the vegetables into the center of each, then place two rolls on top.

4 Seal the parcels tightly and place in a roasting pan. Bake for 15–20 minutes, until the fish is just tender.

5 To serve, open up the parcels, then sprinkle with the basil leaves and grind over a little black pepper.

Skate with Lemon and Capers

Skate wings served with a sharp, herby sauce make a different – and very easy – main course.

INGREDIENTS

Serves 4
4 small skate wings, about
  6–8oz each
seasoned flour
6 tbsp olive oil
1 garlic clove, crushed
finely grated rind of ½ lemon
juice of 1 large lemon
2 tbsp capers, rinsed, drained and
  chopped
2 tbsp chopped fresh flat leaf
  parsley
1 tbsp chopped fresh basil
1 tbsp snipped fresh chives
salt and black pepper

1 Lightly dust the skate wings in the seasoned flour. Heat 2 tbsp of the oil in a large frying pan and, when hot, add the skate wings and fry for 8–10 minutes, turning once, until the flesh begins to part easily from the bone and looks creamy white.

2 Meanwhile, mix together the remaining oil, the garlic, lemon rind and juice in a bowl with the capers, parsley, basil, chives and seasoning.

3 Pour the sauce into the pan to warm it through. Transfer the skate to warmed serving plates and serve with the sauce spooned over the top.

Spanish-style Hake

Cod and haddock cutlets will work just as well as hake in this tasty fish dish.

Ingredients

Serves 4
2 tbsp olive oil
2 tbsp butter
1 onion, chopped
3 garlic cloves, crushed
1 tbsp flour
½ tsp paprika
4 hake steaks, about 6oz each
8oz fine green beans, cut into
   1in lengths
1½ cups fresh fish stock
⅔ cup dry white wine
2 tbsp dry sherry
16–20 live mussels, cleaned
3 tbsp chopped fresh parsley
salt and black pepper
crusty bread, to serve

1 Heat the oil and butter in a sauté or frying pan, add the onion and cook for 5 minutes, until softened, but not browned. Add the crushed garlic and cook for 1 minute more.

2 Mix together the flour and paprika, then lightly dust over the hake steaks. Push the onion and garlic over to one side of the pan.

3 Add the hake steaks to the pan and fry until golden on both sides. Stir in the beans, stock, wine, sherry and seasoning. Bring to a boil and cook for about 2 minutes.

4 Add the mussels and parsley, cover the pan and cook for 5–8 minutes, until the mussels have opened.

5 Serve the hake in warmed, shallow soup bowls with plenty of crusty bread to mop up the juices.

Monkfish with Mexican Salsa

INGREDIENTS

Serves 4

1½lb monkfish tail
3 tbsp olive oil
2 tbsp lime juice
1 garlic clove, crushed
1 tbsp chopped fresh coriander
salt and black pepper
coriander sprigs and lime slices,
  to garnish

For the salsa

4 tomatoes, peeled, seeded and diced
1 avocado, peeled, pitted and diced
½ red onion, chopped
1 green chili, seeded and chopped
2 tbsp chopped fresh coriander
2 tbsp olive oil
1 tbsp lime juice

1 To make the salsa, mix the salsa ingredients and leave at room temperature for about 30 minutes.

2 Prepare the monkfish. Using a sharp knife, remove the pinkish-grey membrane. Cut the fillets from either side of the backbone, then cut each fillet in half to give four steaks.

3 Mix together the oil, lime juice, garlic, coriander and seasoning in a shallow non-metallic dish. Add the monkfish steaks to the dish. Turn the monkfish several times to coat with the marinade, then cover the dish and leave to marinate at cool room temperature, or in the fridge, for 30 minutes.

4 Remove the monkfish from the marinade and broil for 10–12 minutes, turning once and brushing regularly with the marinade until cooked through.

5 Serve the monkfish garnished with coriander sprigs and lime slices and accompanied by the salsa.

COOK'S TIP

It is important to remove the tough pinkish-grey membrane covering the monkfish tail before cooking, otherwise it will shrink and toughen the monkfish.

Tuna with Pan-fried Tomatoes

INGREDIENTS

Serves 2

2 tuna steaks, about 6oz each
6 tbsp olive oil
2 tbsp lemon juice
2 garlic cloves, chopped
1 tsp chopped fresh thyme
4 canned anchovy fillets, drained and
   finely chopped
8oz plum tomatoes, halved
2 tbsp chopped fresh parsley
4–6 black olives, pitted and chopped
black pepper
crusty bread, to serve

— COOK'S TIP —

If you are unable to find fresh tuna steaks, you could replace them with salmon fillets, if you like – just cook them for one or two minutes more on each side.

---

1 Place the tuna steaks in a shallow non-metallic dish. Mix 4 tbsp of the oil with the lemon juice, garlic, thyme, anchovies and pepper. Pour this mixture over the tuna and then leave to marinate for at least 1 hour.

2 Lift the tuna from the marinade and place on a broiling rack. Broil for 4 minutes on each side, or until the tuna feels firm to touch, basting with the marinade. Take care not to overcook.

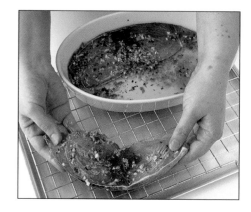

3 Meanwhile, heat the remaining oil in a frying pan. Add the tomatoes and fry for 2 minutes only on each side.

4 Divide the tomatoes equally between two serving plates and scatter over the chopped parsley and olives. Top each with a tuna steak.

5 Add the remaining marinade to the pan juices and warm through. Pour over the tomatoes and tuna steaks and serve at once with crusty bread for mopping up the juices.

Salmon with Herb Butter

INGREDIENTS

Serves 4

4 tbsp butter, softened
finely grated rind of ½ small lemon
1 tbsp lemon juice
1 tbsp chopped fresh dill
4 salmon steaks
2 lemon slices, halved
4 fresh dill sprigs
salt and black pepper

1 Place the butter, lemon rind, lemon juice, chopped dill and seasoning in a small bowl and mix together with a fork until blended.

2 Spoon the butter on to a piece of waxed paper and roll up, smoothing with your hands into a sausage shape. Twist the ends tightly, wrap in plastic wrap and pop in the freezer for 20 minutes, until firm.

COOK'S TIP

Other fresh herbs could be used to flavor the butter – try chopped mint, fennel fronds, lemon balm, parsley or oregano instead of the dill.

---

3 Meanwhile, preheat the oven to 375°F. Cut out four squares of foil big enough to encase the salmon steaks and grease lightly. Place a salmon steak in the center of each one.

4 Remove the butter from the freezer and slice into eight rounds. Place two rounds on top of each salmon steak with a halved lemon slice in the center and a sprig of dill on top. Lift up the edges of the foil and crinkle them together until well sealed.

5 Lift the parcels on to a baking sheet and bake for about 20 minutes. Remove from the oven and place the unopened parcels on warmed plates. Open the parcels and slide the contents on to the plates with the juices.

Char-broiled Squid

INGREDIENTS

Serves 4
2lb squid, cleaned
6 tbsp olive oil
juice of 1–2 lemons
3 garlic cloves, crushed
¼ tsp hot red pepper flakes
4 tbsp chopped fresh parsley
lemon slices, to garnish

1 Reserve the squid tentacles, then using a small sharp knife, score the flesh into a diagonal pattern.

2 Place all the squid in a shallow non-metallic dish. To make the marinade, mix together the olive oil, lemon juice, crushed garlic and hot red pepper flakes in a small bowl.

3 Pour the marinade over the squid and leave in a cool place for at least 2 hours, stirring occasionally.

4 Lift the squid from the marinade and grill for 2 minutes on each side, turning them frequently and brushing with the marinade until the outside is golden brown and crisp, with soft, moist flesh inside.

5 Bring the remaining marinade to a boil in a small pan, stir in the chopped parsley, then pour over the squid. Garnish with lemon wedges and serve at once.

— COOK'S TIP —

If you are in a rush, it is still worth marinating the squid – even for 20 minutes – as this will both tenderize and flavor it.

Monkfish Brochettes

INGREDIENTS

Serves 4
1½lb monkfish, skinned and boned
12 rashers lean bacon
2 small zucchini
1 yellow or orange bell pepper, seeded and cut into 1in cubes

For the marinade
6 tbsp olive oil
grated rind of ½ lime
3 tbsp lime juice
2 tbsp dry white wine
4 tbsp chopped fresh mixed herbs, such as dill, chives and parsley
1 tsp honey
black pepper
saffron rice, to serve

1 To make the marinade, mix together the olive oil, lime rind and juice, wine, chopped herbs, honey and pepper in a bowl, then set aside.

2 Cut the monkfish into 24 x 1in cubes. Stretch the bacon rashers with the back of a knife, then cut each piece in half and wrap around the monkfish cubes.

3 Pare narrow strips of peel from the zucchini to give a striped effect, then cut into 1in chunks.

4 Thread the fish rolls on to skewers alternately with the zucchini and pepper. Place in a dish. Pour over the marinade and leave in a cool place for 1 hour. Lift out the skewers, then grill for about 10 minutes, turning and basting occasionally with the marinade. Serve hot with saffron rice.

Seared Salmon with Mint Salsa

A little piece of salmon treated like this can go a surprisingly long way, with little or no effort. It is good with cod, too.

INGREDIENTS

Serves 4
2 large extra tasty tomatoes, peeled, seeded and diced
3in piece of cucumber, peeled and diced
1 tsp balsamic or red wine vinegar
2 tbsp chopped fresh mint, or 2 tsp dried
3 tbsp olive oil
4 salmon tail fillet pieces (about 1lb in all), or 1 tail piece which you will need to fillet yourself
2 tbsp butter
squeeze of lemon juice
salt and black pepper

1 To make the salsa, mix the diced tomatoes, cucumber, vinegar, mint and 1–2 tbsp olive oil together and season to taste. Chill.

2 Lay the fish between sheets of wax paper and gently bash with a rolling pin, to make them as flat as possible. Brush both sides with oil and season with salt and black pepper.

3 Heat half the butter in a non-stick frying pan and, when really hot, fry the fillets two at a time. Allow only about 1 minute each side and serve at once with a squeeze of lemon juice and the chilled salsa.

Roast Cod with Mixed Beans

INGREDIENTS

Serves 4
4 thick cod steaks
3 tbsp sweet sherry or Madeira
14oz can spicy mixed beans, drained
14oz kidney, borlotti or cannelini beans, drained
2 garlic cloves, crushed
1 tbsp olive oil
1 tsp grated orange rind
1 tbsp chopped fresh parsley
salt and black pepper

1 Skin the steaks, then pour over the sherry or Madeira and leave in a bowl, turning once, for 10 minutes.

2 Preheat the oven to 400°F. Mix the beans with the garlic and place in the base of an ovenproof dish. Place the fish on top and pour over the sherry or Madeira. Brush the fish with the oil, sprinkle with orange rind, half the parsley and seasoning.

3 Cover tightly with foil and cook for 15–20 minutes. Pierce the thickest part of the fish with a knife to check if it is cooked through and continue cooking for only another 2–3 minutes if necessary.

4 Baste the fish with a little of the juices which will have risen to the top of the beans. Then sprinkle with the rest of the parsley just before serving.

INDEX